BIKE
REPAIR
MANUAL

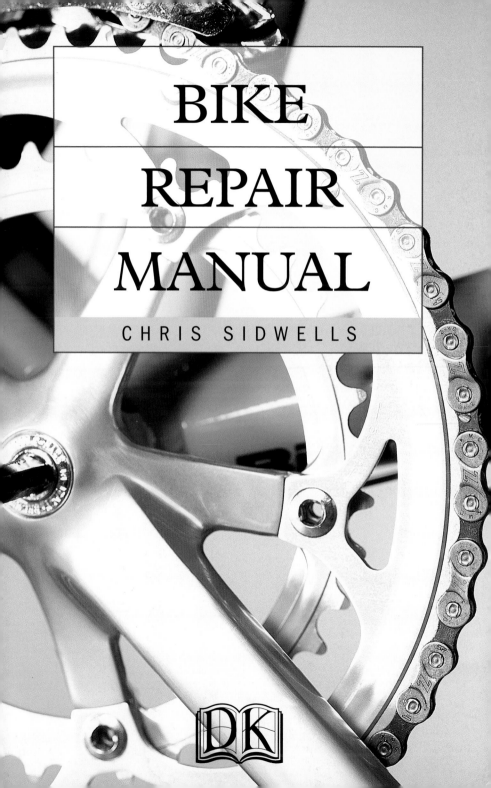

BIKE
REPAIR
MANUAL

CHRIS SIDWELLS

DK

LONDON, NEW YORK, MUNICH,
MELBOURNE, DELHI

Project Editor Richard Gilbert
Senior Art Editor Kevin Ryan
Art Editor Michael Duffy

Managing Editor Adèle Hayward
Managing Art Editor Karen Self

Category Publisher Stephanie Jackson
Art Director Peter Luff

DTP Designers Rajen Shah,
Adam Shepherd
Production Controller Kevin Ward

Produced for Dorling Kindersley by
Editor Pip Morgan
Designer Edward Kinsey

Photographer Gerard Brown
Technical Consultant Guy Andrews

First published in 2004 by
Dorling Kindersley Limited
80 Strand, London WC2R 0RL

A Penguin Company

2 4 6 8 10 9 7 5 3 1

A CIP catalogue record for this book is available
from the British Library.

ISBN 1 4053 0253 4

Reproduced by Colourscan in Singapore
Printed and bound by Star Standard in
Singapore

See our complete catalogue at
www.dk.com

Contents

Introduction

A clean, well-maintained bike will work efficiently and safely, and add to your enjoyment of cycling by giving you peace of mind.

Safety and efficiency are closely linked. If your gears are not shifting correctly, for instance, they will not only affect your riding efficiency, but also tempt you to look down at them while riding to see what is causing the problem. As a result, you might take your eyes off what is happening on the road ahead and expose yourself to the possibility of a collision. The *Bike Repair Manual* will help you avoid such problems by demonstrating how to maintain your bike regularly and correctly.

Understanding technology

Modern bikes may seem complicated and the technology that manufacturers use may be more sophisticated than ever. However, cycle components work, as they have always done, according to logical principles, so there is no reason for you to be daunted.

Before you begin to service a particular component of your bike, first become familiar with the part by turning to the relevant section. Knowing how a part works makes it easier to maintain.

Above all, be confident and patient with what you are doing. Even if you do not think of yourself as mechanically minded, you may come to enjoy bike maintenance after a time and will certainly enjoy the trouble-free cycling that rewards your efforts.

Collecting information

If you buy a new bike, make sure that you keep the accompanying owner's manual, so that you can to refer to it alongside this book. Do the same with any new equipment that you buy.

If your bike is not new, obtain a manual from a bike shop or the manufacturer's web site. Manuals will help you to be aware of the particular maintenance requirements of all the components on your bike.

If you want to learn more about bike mechanics, there are many magazines available that contain tips on specific components. However, the large majority of people who are simply interested in learning how to maintain their bike will find everything they need to know in the pages of the *Bike Repair Manual*.

Using this book

The different maintenance requirements of the most common types of bike are listed at the beginning of the book. These requirements are covered in the step-by-step pages that are specific to the components fitted to each type of bike – for example, suspension forks for mountain bikes.

You will also find a timetable for servicing the parts of your bike and a troubleshooting chart to help you identify and solve problems. The book helps you to spot danger signs and to carry out routine safety checks. These features detail what you need to do and refer you to the relevant step-by-step sequences to explain how to do it.

GETTING TO

KNOW YOUR BIKE

Understanding your bike will make it easier to maintain. Identify all the different parts and components to help you see how they work together as a whole.

The basic bike

Modern bikes, such as the hybrid bike (*below*), are designed to be light and user-friendly. The parts can be grouped into different categories, each performing a key function in the overall operation of the bike.

The frame is the skeleton of the bike, on to which all components are fitted. The fork holds the front wheel, and connects to the handlebar to allow the bike to be steered. The drivetrain is the system that transfers the rider's energy, via the pedals and cranks, to the rear wheel. It also contains a number of cogs, known as chainrings and sprockets, which carry the chain.

The mechs (also known as derailleurs) change gear by moving the chain on to different chainrings and sprockets. They are controlled by the gear-shifters, which are mounted on the handlebar to allow quick and easy use by the rider. The brakes

Hybrid bike ▶
Advances in technology have refined the design and improved the performance of each category of bike part, producing a machine that is easy to ride and maintain.

Frame (*see pp.12–13*)
Improved welding techniques allow thin-walled aluminium tubes to provide a relatively cheap, light and responsive frame. The thickness of the tube walls varies to cope with areas of increased stress.

Wheel (*see pp.98–9, 104–9*)
The rim's shape and high-tech aluminium increases the wheel's strength. The wheel requires fewer spokes, which reduces weight and air resistance.

Mech (*see pp.50–5*)
Mechs are designed to cope with the wide range of sprocket sizes required to climb and descend the steepest hills.

Drivetrain (*see pp.56–77*)
Stiff materials maximize the amount of power the drivetrain transfers to the rear wheel. A triple chainset increases gear range and a flexible chain allows quick, easy gear-shifts.

Pedal (*see pp.78–85*)
Toe-clips and straps give increased power transfer to the pedals, and allow feet to be removed quickly.

are controlled by brake levers that are also mounted on the handlebar, and use brake pads to press against the wheel's rim to bring the bike to a stop.

High-tech machine ▶
Many years of design refinement have produced an adaptable hybrid bike, which combines technology from road and mountain bikes for use in an urban environment.

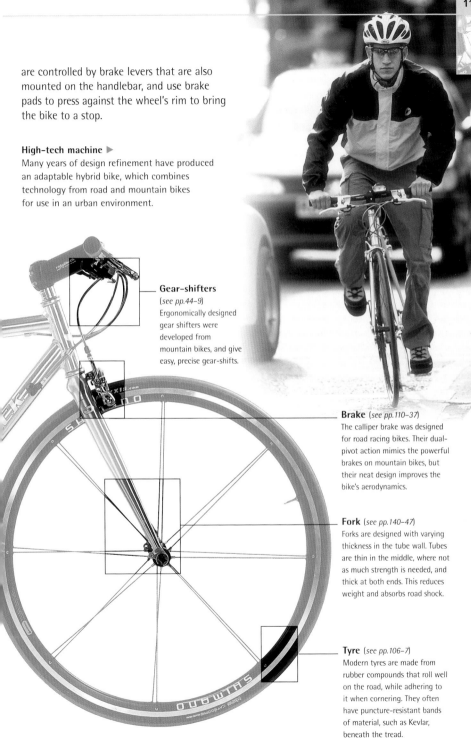

Gear-shifters
(*see pp.44–9*)
Ergonomically designed gear shifters were developed from mountain bikes, and give easy, precise gear-shifts.

Brake (*see pp.110–37*)
The calliper brake was designed for road racing bikes. Their dual-pivot action mimics the powerful brakes on mountain bikes, but their neat design improves the bike's aerodynamics.

Fork (*see pp.140–47*)
Forks are designed with varying thickness in the tube wall. Tubes are thin in the middle, where not as much strength is needed, and thick at both ends. This reduces weight and absorbs road shock.

Tyre (*see pp.106–7*)
Modern tyres are made from rubber compounds that roll well on the road, while adhering to it when cornering. They often have puncture-resistant bands of material, such as Kevlar, beneath the tread.

Anatomy of the bike

Understanding how the parts on your bike fit together will help you perform maintenance tasks successfully. Although your bike may differ from the modern mountain bike (*right*), all bikes fit together in a similar way. For example, the quick-release levers on the wheels below perform the same function as axle nuts on a bike with hub gears.

The main parts and their components, and where each part is attached to the bike, are shown on the mountain bike. Take the time to study the illustration, since it will act as a useful reference to help you follow the steps later in the book.

Mountain bike ▶
The mountain bike is a good example of how parts fit together since it has a similar frame, wheels, drivetrain, pedals, mechs, brakes, and gear-shifters to road and hybrid bikes.

Saddle
Saddle cover
Saddle rails

Seat post
Saddle clamp

Rear brake
Cable-guide tube
Braking surface
Brake pad
Brake arm

Frame
Seat tube
Seat stay
Chainstay
Down tube

Rear hub
Rear drop-out
Hub
Quick-release

Bottom bracket

Cassette
Cassette body
Sprocket
Locknut

Rear mech
Jockey wheel
Mech plate
Barrel adjuster

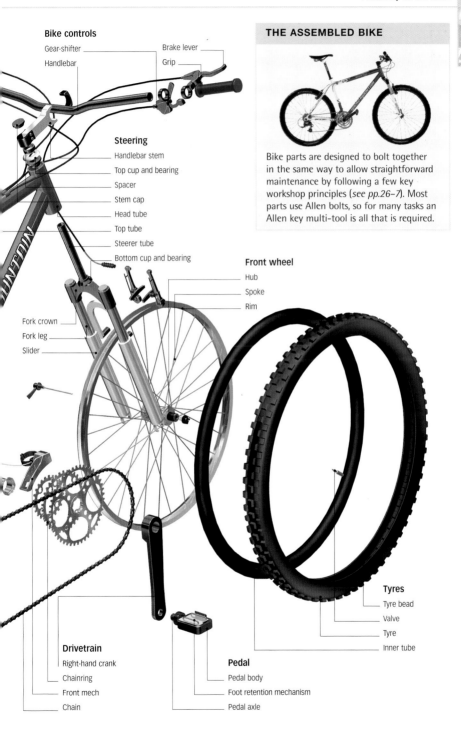

Bike controls

Gear-shifter

Handlebar

Brake lever

Grip

THE ASSEMBLED BIKE

Bike parts are designed to bolt together in the same way to allow straightforward maintenance by following a few key workshop principles (*see pp.26–7*). Most parts use Allen bolts, so for many tasks an Allen key multi-tool is all that is required.

Steering

Handlebar stem

Top cup and bearing

Spacer

Stem cap

Head tube

Top tube

Steerer tube

Bottom cup and bearing

Fork crown

Fork leg

Slider

Front wheel

Hub

Spoke

Rim

Tyres

Tyre bead

Valve

Tyre

Inner tube

Drivetrain

Right-hand crank

Chainring

Front mech

Chain

Pedal

Pedal body

Foot retention mechanism

Pedal axle

Bikes for general use

You can buy a bike for almost every purpose imaginable but a simple utility, hybrid, or folding bike will still increase your fitness, save you money on fares, and make no negative impact on your environment.

As long as the bike is of good quality, you will only need to keep it clean and check it regularly for signs of wear. Hybrid bikes, utility bikes, and folding bikes are all dependable machines that are suited to commuting to work or school, day-to-day transport needs, or simply a pleasurable ride in the park or even the countryside.

The hybrid bike
Lightweight materials combined with road bike performance and hardy mountain bike technology make hybrid bikes perfect for bumpy urban roads. They are ideal for commuting, family rides, fitness riding, touring, and carrying luggage.

The utility bike
Utility bikes are ideal for local commuting and short rides. They are equipped with fat tyres that absorb road bumps but will drag on long journeys, making them hard work to ride and uncomfortable.

The folding bike
Ideal for commuters, and for people with little space in which to store a standard bike, folding bikes can go anywhere, especially on public transport. The folded bike can be easily reassembled into a serviceable machine without the use of tools.

Urban commuting
With its head-up, traffic-friendly riding position and easy-to-operate gears, the lightweight hybrid is ideal for urban commuting.

ESSENTIAL MAINTENANCE CHECKLIST

HYBRID BIKE

• Regularly maintain and lubricate the derailleur gears (*see pp.52–3, 54–5*).
• Check the gear cables for signs of wear (*see p.39, pp.48–9*).
• Check the brake cables for signs of wear (*see p.39, pp.116–17*).
• Check the tyres for signs of wear (*see p.39*).
• Regularly change the chain (*see pp.64–5*).

Tyre
Rear mech
Front mech
Brake cable
Gear cable
Chain

UTILITY BIKE

• Regularly lubricate the hub gears (*see pp.58–9, 60–1*).
• Regularly check the gear cables for signs of wear (*see p.39*).
• Regularly check the brake control cables for signs of wear (*pp.116–17*).
• Regularly check the brake pads for signs of wear (*see p.38*).
• Regularly clean and grease the chain (*see pp.28–9, 30–1*).

Sprung saddle
Brake lever
Handlebar basket
Hub gears
Chainguard

FOLDING BIKE

• Regularly check and lubricate the pivots and the locks that allow the bike to fold and unfold.
• Regularly check hub gears, even though they are shielded from the elements and so need very little maintenance (*see pp.58–9, 60–1*)
• Pay extra attention to the outer control cables (*see p.39, pp.48–9*).

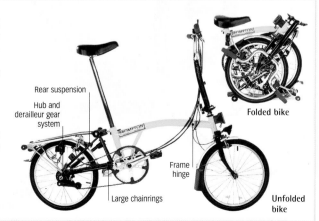

Rear suspension
Hub and derailleur gear system
Frame hinge
Large chainrings
Folded bike
Unfolded bike

Specialist bikes

If you want to take up cycling as a sport or hobby, rather than simply as a means of transport, look for a more specialized bike, such as a race level road bike, a mountain bike, or a BMX bike.

As bikes become more sophisticated they need more care. For example, lightweight parts wear quickly, so they must be kept scrupulously clean. Carbon wheel rims require special brake pads that do not work well on metal. Hydraulic disc brakes and suspension systems need regular attention.

Do not let this put you off buying your dream bike. Just as riding it will be a joy, maintaining it to exacting standards will be part of the whole cycling experience.

The road bike
Lightweight materials and narrow tyres make road bikes good for fitness riding, day touring, and competitions. The aerodynamic position afforded by a drop handlebar offers great speed. Road bikes are so light and have such a range of gears that almost anyone, with a little training, can tackle the great mountain passes made famous by the Tour de France.

The mountain bike
Full-suspension mountain bikes allow you to break new ground and ride across rugged terrain that was previously unthinkable and at speeds that were once unattainable.

The BMX bike
These bikes are built for acceleration and agile bike handling. Like some of the very first bikes, BMXs are made almost entirely from steel because it transfers power in a way that no other material can.

Road riding
This road bike represents the ultimate in road bike design, and is the type of bike that professionals use in the Tour de France.

ESSENTIAL MAINTENANCE CHECKLIST

ROAD BIKE

- Regularly clean and lubricate the bike (see pp.28–9, 30–1).
- Make routine safety checks (see pp.32–3).
- Check the brakes (see pp.118–19).
- Check the gears are working perfectly (see pp.52–3, 54–5).
- Where carbon-fibre components fit inside other components, cover their joints with copper-based anti-seize (see pp.30–1).

Calliper brake

20-speed gear-shift system

Aluminium/carbon-fibre frame

Aluminium drop handlebar

Road race tyre

Clipless pedal

MOUNTAIN BIKE

- Set up the suspension system (see pp.142-43, 150–51).
- Regularly clean and lubricate the suspension (see pp.144–45, 146–47).
- Inspect all pivots and seals regularly.
- Check brake cables and pads regularly (see pp.38–3, pp.116–17).
- Replace the cassette every six months (see pp.66–7).
- Service the headset regularly (see pp.90–1, 92–3).

Rear V-brake

Rear derailleur

Aluminium frame

Carbon-fibre straight handlebar

Cross-country tyre

Rear shock

Short-travel suspension fork

BMX BIKE

- Regularly check the bottom bracket to see that it is running free, but not loose (see pp.76–7).
- Replace the pedals if their axles are bent (see pp.80–1).
- Adjust the brakes to ensure the minimum of travel before the brakes come on, as the steel rims, though very strong, do not make good braking surfaces (see pp.124–25).

Single gearing

Gyro headset

Stunt peg

Opposite transmission

Setting up an adult's bike

If the saddle's height and angle are adjusted and the position of the brake levers on the handlebar is set so that they are within easy reach, then riding will be more efficient and comfortable. A novice cyclist should try setting the saddle height a little lower at first, and work towards the ideal once he or she is used to riding.

STEP LOCATOR

Toolbox
- Allen key multi-tool ● Spanners
- Screwdriver

Adjusting your riding position

Remove your shoes and sit on your bike, supporting yourself against a wall.

● Set your cranks so that the pedal furthest from the wall is at the low point of its revolution.

● Put the heel of your foot on the pedal. Your leg should be straight when you do this. Ask someone to help you check.

The knee aligns with the axle

Place the widest part of your foot over the pedal axle. If your shoes have cleats, set them up so that your foot can easily adopt this position (see pp.84–5).

● Set your cranks parallel to the floor. The depression on the side of your leading leg, just behind the kneecap, should be directly over the axle of the pedal. Ask your helper to check.

Move your saddle back if the depression on your leg is in front of the axle. If it is behind, move it forwards.

● Undo the saddle clamp under the saddle. On modern bikes, you will need an Allen key; on older bikes, use a spanner.

● Repeat Steps 4 and 5 until you are sure you have the position right.

2 **Raise the saddle** if your leg is not straight when your heel is on the pedal. Lower the saddle if your heel does not reach the pedal.

● Undo the seat pin clamp bolt. Raise or lower the saddle, tighten up the bolt, and try again. Ask your helper to see if your leg is straight. Do not lean on the foot that you are testing.

3 **To make absolutely sure** the saddle height is right for you, go for a ride with your cycling shoes on and your feet in their normal position on the pedals.

● Ask your helper to ride behind you and check that your hips are not rocking from side to side as you ride. If they are, the saddle is set too high and you need to repeat Steps 1 and 2.

6 **Adjust the reach** of the brake levers if you have small hands and short fingers.

● Undo the brakes and screw in the adjuster on each brake lever until you can reach the lever easily. Then reset the brakes.

● Set the brake levers at an angle to the handlebar so that you can pull them in line with your arm.

7 **Make sure that the brake reach** allows you to apply the brakes using the first joints of your first two fingers, while holding the handlebar securely with your thumb and remaining fingers. You should be able to hook your fingers over the brake levers. If you have to stretch too far, you will be unable to apply the correct power.

Setting up a child's bike

Before a child starts riding a bike, adjust the saddle and handlebar to suit his or her body. Set the saddle at its lowest point, as in Step 1. Buy the biggest bike possible at first, then keep adjusting it as the child grows taller. Children's bikes are usually measured by wheel size – from 30cm (12in) up to 60cm (24in).

STEP LOCATOR

Toolbox
- Allen key multi-tool ● Spanners
- Plastic mallet

Adjusting the position of the saddle

1 **Set the saddle** on your child's bike at a height that allows him or her to sit on it and simultaneously to touch the ground with the front part of each foot. This is the ideal set-up.

Adjusting the height of the handlebar

1 **Raise or lower the bike's handlebar** by loosening the expander bolt that holds the stem into the bike. This bolt is secured by either an Allen bolt or a hexagonal bolt, so use an Allen key or a spanner to loosen it.

● Knock the bolt down with a plastic mallet to free it up if you need to.

2 **Grip the front wheel** between your legs to steady it and then pull the handlebar up or push it down. Do not pull the handlebar higher than the safety limit that is marked on the stem. Once the handlebar is at the right height, and the stem is lined up with the front wheel, tighten the expander bolt.

2 **Loosen the seat pin clamp** – it either has a quick-release lever or a nut-and-bolt fixing that requires a spanner. Either pull the saddle up or push it down to the required height.

3 **Move the saddle** forwards or backwards by loosening the nut that secures the seat clamp. Tighten the nut again, but be sure that the saddle is horizontal to the ground.

3 **Adjust the saddle** and handlebar still further if you need to, so that your child can sit in the ideal riding position – neither too upright, nor too stretched.

CARING FOR YOUR BIKE

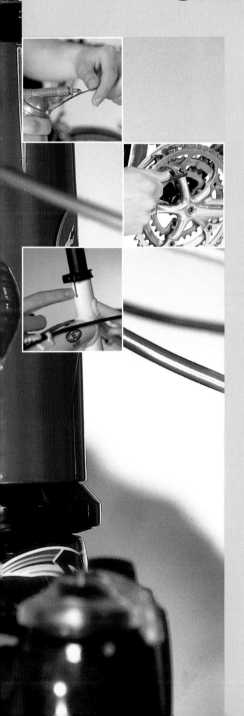

Your bike needs to be kept clean and well lubricated to avoid mechanical problems. Learning to make cleaning, lubricating, and checking a regular part of your bike routine will lengthen the life of your bike and its components.

Tools

If you are going to regularly maintain and repair your bike, you will need to buy a toolkit or assemble your own. The tools shown opposite will enable you to carry out all the essential repairs and to maintain your bike at peak performance. Add other tools as the need arises when specific parts of your bike require maintenance or replacing. However, try to follow a few general principles when using the tools.

When using tools on a bike, especially lightweight bikes, you need a delicate touch. If you are used to working on cars, then use less force when dealing with your bike. Nuts and bolts only need to be tight; if you over-tighten them they will shear. If in doubt, buy torque gauges that accurately measure the correct level of tightness on a bike's nuts and bolts. See the component manufacturers' instructions for recommended torque settings. In fact, it is essential to keep all the instructions that come with your bike, tools, and any components you buy.

Buy the best-quality, precision-made tools. They will last for many years if you look after them. Cheap tools will bend and become chipped, making it impossible to carry out some maintenance jobs properly. They could even damage the components that you work on.

Working with tools
When using your tools to maintain or repair your bike, give yourself plenty of room and always work in a tidy, well-lit environment.

Essential toolkits

Start your toolkit with the two multi-tools, the spanners to fit the cones, long-nosed pliers, cable cutters, a pump, and a workstand.

Pumps and Workstand

Workstand

Frame-fitting pump

Shock pump

Track pump

Spanners and Allen Keys

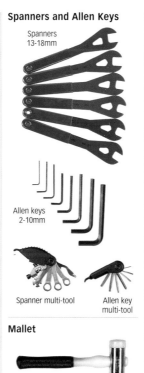

Spanners 13-18mm

Allen keys 2-10mm

Spanner multi-tool

Allen key multi-tool

Mallet

Plastic mallet

Transmission Tools

Crank-bolt remover

Chain whip

Crank puller

Chain tool

Cassette remover

Bottom Bracket Tools

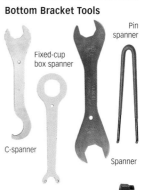

Pin spanner

Fixed-cup box spanner

Spanner

C-spanner

Bottom-bracket remover

Pliers and Cable Cutters

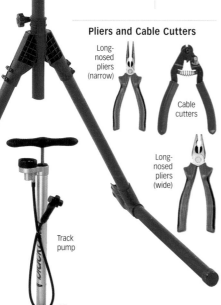

Long-nosed pliers (narrow)

Cable cutters

Long-nosed pliers (wide)

SPECIALIST TOOLS

Some maintenance and replacement tasks require specialist tools that you will not use very often. Other tools, such as the cable puller, are not essential but will make some jobs easier.

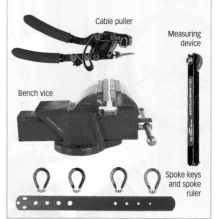

Cable puller

Measuring device

Bench vice

Spoke keys and spoke ruler

Workshop principles

Four key principles govern the work on your bike. The most useful is tidiness – find a place for each tool and return it there when you have finished with it. Second, do not use too much force to tighten components – the nuts and bolts of lightweight parts can easily shear. Third, remember the order in which you take components apart. Finally, keep all of your tools clean and dry.

The guidelines below provide you with general principles for some of the most common tools or operations in bike repair.

Using Allen keys

Put the long axis of an Allen key in the Allen bolt to make the key easier to use, both for repeated turns and in places where space is tight or restricted, such as putting a bottle cage on the down tube.

Use the short axis of an Allen key to make the final turn when tightening an Allen bolt – for example, on a chainring. You can also use this technique to start undoing an Allen bolt.

Using pliers

Use long-nosed pliers to hold cables and keep them under tension. Buy a small pair with pointed jaws for tight areas. Keep the jaws clean and grease-free. Lubricate the pivot with light oil occasionally.

Fix a cable tidy on to a brake cable to stop the ends from fraying. Push the cable tidy on to the end of the cable and squeeze it flat with your pliers. If you are gentle, you can use the inside jaws of your cable cutters.

Using a spanner

Always use the correct size of spanner for the nut you are tightening or loosening. Hold the spanner firmly at the end to maximize leverage. Make sure that the jaws fully enclose the nut to prevent it from slipping.

Cutting cable outers

Cut a brake cable outer between the spirals of the metal tube under the sheath. If the spirals become compressed, squeeze them with the inside of your cutter jaws until they are round.

Cut a gear cable outer through the wire under the sheath. If you need to, squeeze the wire with the inside of your cutter jaws until its cross-section is round again.

Organizing a bike workshop

Regularly maintaining your bike and carrying
out essential repairs means that you can keep
your bike at peak performance. If you have the
space, the best place to do this is in a workshop
that is well organized and equipped with all the
tools you need for your particular bike. Create a
workshop that is dry with plenty of light – and
follow the four key workshop principles.

Cleaning your bike

Although a bike is a very efficient and durable machine, some of its more delicate parts are at the mercy of the elements. Grit and dirt, for example, stick to lubricants and act as a grinding agent. Clean the parts regularly to keep them running smoothly and prevent them from wearing out.

While cleaning your bike, check all the parts and components for damage. With the wheels taken out, you can look at parts of the bike's frame that are usually hidden and examine each component for signs of dangerous wear (see pp.32–3 and pp.38–9).

The process of cleaning is straightforward. First remove old lubricants by applying a degreaser. Then wash the dirt off with water and detergent. Finally, rinse, dry, and lubricate the exposed moving parts.

Cleaning equipment
- Plastic bucket ● Sponges ● Degreaser ● Cloth
- Hard-bristled brushes ● Cassette scraper

Removing dirt and oil

1 **Remove both wheels** from the bike and put the frame in a workstand or hang it up.

● Place a chain holder in the rear drop-out to keep the chain tight while the rear wheel is out of the bike. This allows the chain to run freely so that it can be cleaned thoroughly.

● Apply a degreaser to remove any old oil and grit. Spray on to the chainset, front and rear mechs, and the chain, covering each link.

4 **Clean the rest of the wheel,** including the tyres, with a bigger brush and soapy water.

● Work the bristles in between the spokes and around the hub. Rinse with clean water and dry everything with a cloth.

5 **Spray the chainrings,** chainset, and front mech with more degreaser if there is still stubborn oil and dirt (inset).

● Dip the sponge into hot, soapy water and wrap it around the chain. Turn the pedals so the chain runs through the sponge.

● Use the same sponge to wash the rear mech, especially its jockey wheels, the front mech, and the chainrings.

2 **Use a cassette scraper** to gouge out any dirt and debris that has accumulated between the sprockets.

3 **Use a hard-bristled brush** on the cassette so that the degreaser reaches into the spaces between the sprockets. Allow a few minutes for the degreaser to work and wash off with soapy water.

6 **Apply plenty of soapy water** to the rest of the bike with a different sponge. Start at the top and work down.

• Use different-sized, hard-bristled brushes to work the water into the places that are hard to reach.

• Rinse with clean water and dry the bike with a clean cloth.

• Use a sponge to work soap into intricate parts, such as between the brake arms and the pads.

• Replace the wheels and sparingly apply a light oil to the chain and the moving parts of the front and rear mechs.

Lubricating your bike

Regular lubrication helps a bike to run smoothly and prevents excessive wear and tear. Each time a part of the bike is lubricated, remember to remove the old oil and grease with degreaser first (*see pp.28–9*). Applying new lubrication on top of old does not work because lubricants attract grit and dirt to the bike and form a grinding paste that can cause damage.

The lubricants needed vary from light spray oil (dry lube) and heavier oil (wet lube) to light grease manufactured specifically for bikes and anti-seize compounds.

STEP LOCATOR

Applying oil and grease

1 **Dribble some light oil** inside the cable outers before you fit a new cable. This makes sure that the cable runs smoothly inside. Poor gear-shifts are often due to cables running dry inside their outers. The same is true of brakes that are hard to apply and slow to return to the ready-to-use position.

3 **Dribble light oil** on to the pivots in the front and rear mechs once a week. The jockey wheels on the rear mech also need some light oil where they rotate around the jockey wheel bolts.

- Make sure that you flush out any old oil with degreaser first.

4 **Oil the chain** after riding in the wet, and clean, dry, and lubricate when cleaning your bike (*see pp.28–9*). Except in winter, or in bad conditions, use light oil from a spray can or bottle.

- Hold a cloth underneath the chain to catch any excess oil.

5 **Grease open bearings** after regular cleaning with a light grease specifically made for bikes. Bottom brackets and hubs need most attention, but headsets need regreasing less often. Riding regularly in the rain shortens the interval between lubrications.

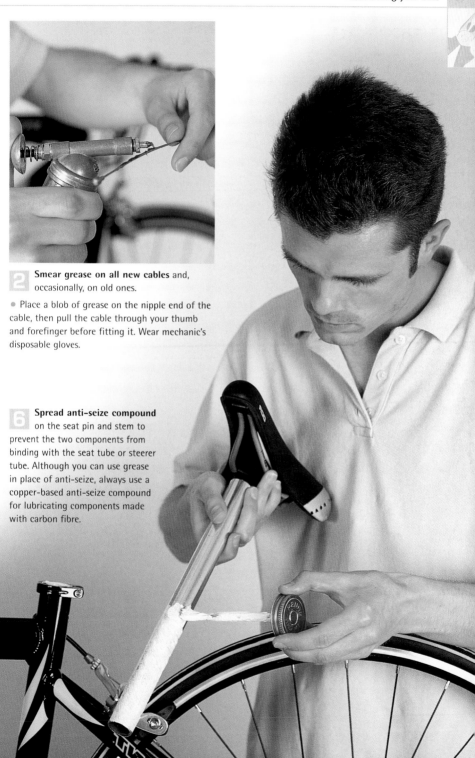

Smear grease on all new cables and, occasionally, on old ones.

● Place a blob of grease on the nipple end of the cable, then pull the cable through your thumb and forefinger before fitting it. Wear mechanic's disposable gloves.

Spread anti-seize compound on the seat pin and stem to prevent the two components from binding with the seat tube or steerer tube. Although you can use grease in place of anti-seize, always use a copper-based anti-seize compound for lubricating components made with carbon fibre.

Making routine safety checks

Every week or so, check the bike frame for signs of wear. Before going for a ride, run through a few checks to reduce the chances of a mechanical failure: brakes that cease to work, a loose handlebar, a tyre blow-out, or slipping gears. The checks will help to avoid many of the accidents caused by equipment failures. Safety checks help the management of a bike, allowing the replacement of parts in good time or the completion of non-urgent maintenance work.

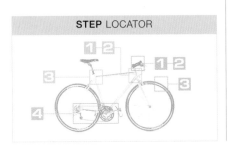

STEP LOCATOR

Making frame checks

1 **Inspect the frame** every week or so and look for metal fatigue. Run a finger under the down tube where it joins the head tube. A ripple in the tube's surface could lead to a break.

● Check around the area where the chainstay bridge is brazed to the chainstays, particularly on a steel frame. Cracks may form in the metal here because of the heat of the brazing process.

Making pre-ride checks

1 **Hold the front wheel** firmly between your legs and try to turn the handlebar from one side to the other. If there is any movement, check the stem and steerer bolts and tighten them if necessary.

● Try twisting the bar upwards to look for rotational movement.

2 **Apply each brake** fully and push the bike forwards. If the lever pulls to the bar before the brake stops a wheel rotating, adjust the travel or replace the pads.

● Apply the front brake. Tighten the headset if you feel any play in the steerer assembly.

3 **Lift the bike,** slowly spin the wheels, and check the tyres for cuts, splits, or bulges. If you find a bulge, or are in any doubt, replace the tyre. Check the tyre pressure.

● Check that all quick-release levers are in the locked position, and wheel nuts are tight.

2 **Monitor all the parts** that are riveted to an aluminium frame, especially the cable guides or the front mech hangers. The rivets form potentially weak areas where stresses in the metal may develop into cracks.

3 **Examine the slot** under the seat-post binder bolt since it can crack on any frame. The slot breaks the seat tube's integrity so that stress can cause a split. To reduce the chances of this happening, always fit a seat post that exactly matches the tube's inside diameter.

4 **Run through the gears** and make sure that they are properly adjusted. Gears that will not mesh properly after you change them can be distracting and, if you look down to see what is wrong, potentially dangerous. If the gears are correctly adjusted and the chain is still jumping, check for a stiff link.

Servicing

Schedule the work you need to carry out on your bike by developing a servicing timetable. The timetable on the right provides a good template since it shows the tasks you should perform on your bike and suggests when you should do them.

Your schedule depends on how much and where your bike is ridden. A heavily-used, off-road bike requires attention at much shorter intervals, whereas a bike used for infrequent, short road journeys will need less regular attention.

However, work carried out as part of a service schedule does not replace the safety checks that must be carried out before every ride (see pp.32–3), or regularly looking for danger signs (see pp.38–9). You should also check your bike and lubricate the transmission every time you clean it.

SERVICING TIMETABLE

EVERY WEEK

TRANSMISSION	CHECK	Chain for wear (see pp.64–5) Gear-shift performance (see pp.46–9, 52–5) Inner cables for fraying and outer cables for wear (see pp.46–9) Cranks and chainring bolts for tightness (see pp.68
	LUBRICATE	Oil chain (see pp.30–1) Oil jockey wheels (see pp.54–5)
	REPLACE	
STEERING AND WHEELS	CHECK	Headset for looseness and ease of steering (see pp.90–3) Action of quick-release levers (see pp.104–5) Wheels for broken spokes and trueness (see pp.108– Handlebar and stem for cracks (see pp.94–7)
	LUBRICATE	
	REPLACE	
BRAKES	CHECK	Inner cables for fraying and and outer cables for w (see pp.114–17) Pads for wear and alignment (see pp.118–25, 128–2 Hydraulic hoses for wear, kinks, or leaks (see pp.130– Brake levers, arms, discs, and callipers for cracks (see pp.114–25, pp.128–33) Disc and calliper bolts for tightness (see pp.130–3
	LUBRICATE	Oil-exposed cables by wiping with wet lube on a ra
	REPLACE	
SUSPENSION	CHECK	Fork and shock exterior surfaces for cracks (see pp.144–47, 150–51) Stanchions under shock boots, if fitted, for cracks (see pp.142–43) Top caps, crown bolts, and shaft bolts for tightness (see pp.140–41, 144–45, 146–47)
	LUBRICATE	Teflon oil on fork stanchions and shock body, and on all seals (see pp.142–47, 150–51)
	REPLACE	

EVERY MONTH

Bottom bracket for smooth running, play, and bent axle (see pp.72–7)
Pedals for play, and clipless pedals for play and release action (see pp.80–3)
Rear mech pivots for play (see pp.54–5)
Sprocket and chainring teeth for wear (see pp.66–9)

Oil mech pivots (see pp.30–1)
Oil and grease inner and outer cables (see pp.30–1)
Oil clipless pedal release mechanisms (see pp.40–1)

Chain on a heavily used bike (see pp.40–1, 64–5)

Hubs for play on axles, roughness, or tight spots (see pp.100–3)
Rubber seals on hubs for splits (see pp.100–3)
Covers, if fitted, on headsets (see pp.40–1)

Oil the seals on hubs (see pp.100–3)

Discs for wear and callipers for alignment (see pp.130–31)
Coaster brake action and chain tension (see pp.136–37)

Grease inner cables and oil inside outer cables (see pp.30–1, 114–17)

Brake pads of heavily used mountain bikes (see pp.120–23)

Fork and shock for play (see pp.142–47, 150–51)
Fork stanchions to see if oil line visible (see pp.142–47)
Fork and shock seals for cracks and slackness (see pp.142–47, 150–51).
Play, absence of oil lines, and cracked seals are all evidence of worn seals, which should be replaced by a qualified technician.
Fork and shock sag (see pp.142–43, 150–51)

Tip bike upside down and store overnight so oil can redistribute in fork

EVERY SIX MONTHS

Freehub body and freewheel for play (see pp.66–7)
Rear mech frame fixing bolt for play (see pp.54–5)
Cleats for wear (see pp.84–5)
Jockey wheels for wear (see pp.54–5)

Grease open-bearing bottom bracket (see pp.74–5)
Oil in hub gear, if equipped with oil port (see pp.58–9)
Grease bearings in pedals (see pp.80–1)

Chain (see pp.64–5)
Inner and outer cables (see pp.46–9)
Sprockets on a heavily used bike (see pp.66–7)

Bearings in open-bearing hubs for wear (see pp.100–1)
Bearings and bearing surfaces in headsets for wear (see pp.90–3)

Grease open-bearing hubs (see pp.100–1)
Grease headsets (see pp.90–3)

Handlebar tape and grips (see pp.94–7)

Grease brake bosses (see pp.122–23)

Inner and outer cables (see pp.114–17)

Fork steerer for cracks, by removing the headset (see pp.90–3)

Fork oil (see pp.144–47)
Seals on forks and shocks, as part of bi-annual service by qualified technician

Troubleshooting

The symptoms of some of the things that can go wrong with your bike are listed in this troubleshooting chart. It explains why a bike may be showing these symptoms and then suggests a solution, referring you to the pages where you will find a detailed sequence of steps to guide you.

   If you still find the problem difficult to solve, consult the How They Work pages for the specific part you are working on, so that you can understand it better. However, sometimes, the symptoms confronting you can be due to a different malfunction to the one suggested in this chart. If after consulting the relevant pages in the book you still cannot solve the problem, ask the experts at a good bike shop for help.

SOLVING COMMON PROBLEM

PROBLEM

TRANSMISSION	The chain will not shift on to a smaller sprocket or chainring.
	The chain will not shift on to a larger sprocket or it shifts but does not run smoothly on it.
	The chain shifts cleanly, but jumps on the sprockets when pressure is applied to the pedals.
	The chain rubs on the inner then the outer side of the front mech cage. On a bike with a single chainring, the chain persistently falls off.
STEERING AND WHEELS	When you apply the front brake and push the bike forwards, the headset moves forwards relative to the head tube.
	You hear a sudden snapping noise come from a wheel while riding and/or the wheel goes out of true.
	There is side-to-side play of a hub on its axle, or when turning the axle in the hub you feel either a roughness or tight and loose spots.
	When pedalling forwards, the cassette spins, but there is no drive to the bike. Alternatively, the cassette spins before the drive is engaged or there is much side-to-side play in the cassette.
BRAKES	The brakes are hard to apply, and/or sluggish to release.
	You have to pull the brake lever a long way before the brakes engage.
	The two brake pads do not contact the braking surface at the same time.
	The brake pads contact the braking surface without pulling the lever too far, but are ineffective at slowing the bike.
SUSPENSION	The fork regularly reaches the limit of its travel (bottoms ou
	On steep, smooth descents, the rear wheel lifts under braking.
	The front wheel judders up and down when cornering.
	A rear air/oil shock regularly reaches the limit of its trave (bottoms out).

CAUSE	SOLUTION
Either grit has become lodged inside the cable outers or the cable lubrication has dried up.	Strip down the cables, flush the outers with degreaser, clean the inners with degreaser, lubricate, and reassemble. (See pp.30–1, 46–9.)
The cable has stretched or the relevant mech is poorly adjusted.	Unclamp the cable at the mech, pull through any slack, and re-tighten. Then set up the mech. (See pp.52–5.)
Either the chain has a stiff link; or the chain or sprockets, or both, are worn; or a chainring may be bent	Check the chain for a stiff link and remove it if found. If no stiff link, replace the chain. If the problem persists, replace the sprockets. If the chainring is bent, replace it. (See pp.62–9.)
The bottom bracket is worn or its axle may be bent.	If the bottom bracket is a cartridge type, replace it. If it is an open-bearing bottom bracket, it may be possible to replace the worn bearings or bent axle. (See pp.72–7.)
The headset is loose or worn.	Strip and inspect the headset. Replace bearings if worn, regrease, and reassemble. Inspect the cups and races; if they are worn you should let a good bike shop replace the whole headset. (See pp.90–3.)
A spoke may have broken.	Replace the spoke and true the wheel. (See pp.108–9.)
The hub bearings are worn or, in the case of tight and loose spots, the axle is bent.	Replace the bearings or the axle. (See pp.100–3.)
The freehub body is worn.	Replace the freehub body. (See pp.100–1.)
Grit and dirt is inside the cable outers or the lubrication on the inner cables has dried.	Strip down the cables, flush the outers, and clean the inner cables with degreaser, lubricate both, and reassemble. (See pp.30–1, 114–17.)
The pads are wearing down or the cable has slipped through the clamp bolt.	If the pads are not too worn, take up the extra travel by unclamping the brakes, pulling the cable through the clamp, and tightening. If the pads are worn, replace them. (See pp.112–25, 128–37.)
Your brakes are not centred.	Follow the procedures for centring the type of brakes on your bike. (See pp.112–25, 128–37.)
There is grease on the pads, foreign bodies embedded in them, or they are wearing unevenly. You may even need a different compound of brake pad.	Rub the pads with emery cloth. Remove foreign bodies with long-nosed pliers. Fit new pads if they are worn unevenly. Seek advice from a bike shop regarding different pad compounds. (See pp.112–25, 128–37.)
With air/oil forks, not enough air is in the system. With coil/oil forks, too light a spring is fitted.	Pump in more air. Replace springs with heavier duty springs. (See pp.142–45.)
The front of the bike is diving under braking because the fork is not stiff enough.	Pump in air, or increase pre-load, according to the type of fork on your bike. (See pp.142–45.)
The fork's rebound is set too fast.	Use the relevant adjuster to reduce the speed of the fork's rebound. (See pp.142–45.)
Insufficient air in the shock, or too much damping, means that the shock is not returning from each compression quickly enough.	Set up the sag on the shock again. If the problem continues, use the damping adjustment to speed up the action of the shock. (See pp.150–51.)

Spotting danger signs

The more you ride your bike, the quicker the various moving parts, particularly tyres and brake pads, will wear away. Replacing the parts as soon as they become worn not only keeps the bike running smoothly but also reduces the chances of an accident. You will save money, too, since worn parts have the knock-on effect of wearing out other parts.

As you run through your safety checks (see pp.32–3), look for worn teeth on sprockets and chainrings, worn brake pads, split or frayed cables, worn wheel rims, bulging or split tyres, and worn tyre treads. If you spot any danger signs, take action as soon as you can. You must replace a damaged part before you next ride your bike.

Checking for wear
Regularly check the tyres, rims, brakes, chainrings, cables, and sprockets so that you can spot signs of wear as early as possible.

Cables

Rims and tyres

Brakes

Sprockets

Chainrings

Sprockets and chainrings
Worn teeth

Regularly check for worn or missing teeth on a chainring or sprocket. The chain can jump when you apply pressure to the pedals, especially if you are out of the saddle, and you may be pitched forwards and crash. Replace the chainring or sprocket as soon as you see this sign (see pp.66–9).

Brakes
Worn brake pads

Regularly check all the brake pads for uneven wear. This is a sign that they are not contacting the braking surface evenly. The effectiveness of your brakes is compromised, because not all the pad's surface is in use. Fit new pads and adjust your brakes correctly (see pp.120–25).

Cables
Split or frayed cables

Check all cables and cable outers for signs of
splitting and fraying. Frayed inner cables can snap,
leaving you without gears, which is inconvenient,
or without brakes, which is dangerous. Change the
cable before you ride again (*see pp.46–9, 114–17*).
Worn or split outers reduce the effectiveness of
your brakes and allow dirt to get in and clog the
cables. Change the outer as soon as you can.

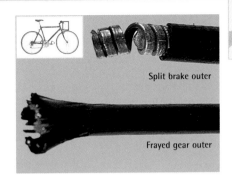

Split brake outer

Frayed gear outer

Rims and tyres
Worn rim

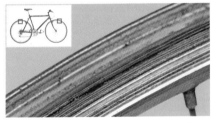

Look for evidence of deep scoring on the rims
of each of your bike's wheels. Rim brakes will
gradually wear out the rims, especially if you ride
off-road or in winter. Eventually, the rims will fail
and you could crash. Cracks around the nipples of
the spokes where they join the rim are a danger
sign, too. Replace the rim if you see these signs.

Bulging tyre

Check the whole circumference of both tyres
for bulges in the tread or the walls. Tyres with
bulges or distortions are very likely to blow out
if you ride on them. If you see any of these signs,
replace the tyre (*see pp.106–7*).

Split tyre

Check each tyre for splits or cuts in the tread or
side walls. A large split means that the internal
fabric of the tyre is damaged, so the tyre is likely
to blow out. Smaller splits and cuts will let sharp
objects penetrate the tyre, causing at least a
puncture and possibly a rapid blow-out. Replace
the tyre if you see any splits or cuts (*see pp.106–7*).

Worn tread

Look closely at the tread of both tyres for signs
of wear. If the tread is worn, the tyre has lost
structural strength and can break down and
distort or bulge. The result can be a blow-out
during the course of a single ride. A tyre that has
been skidded and lost enough rubber to develop a
flat spot can also be dangerous. Replace the tyre
if you see either sign (*see pp.106–7*).

Preparing for wet weather

These steps will help you to prepare a bike for the rigours of winter, a particularly wet climate, or if most of your riding is done off-road. The mud, sand, and water that your wheels spray up into every part of the bike combine to form a damaging, grinding paste. Salt, often used to treat roads where ice is likely to occur, will quickly corrode your bike. Regular cleaning and lubricating helps with protection, but try to stop the mud and salt from reaching the delicate parts of the bike in the first place. The overall aim when protecting a bike in winter is to prevent water reaching non-exposed parts and stopping water from washing off the lubricant on exposed parts.

Protecting a bike
Fit mudguards, insert seals, and lubricate the exposed parts to protect a bike from wet conditions.

Mudguard

Headset

Mech

Seat post collar

Pedal

Chain

Shielding exposed components

Sealing the seat post collar

Keep water out of the point where the seat pin enters the frame. Mark this junction and remove the pin. Pull a piece of narrow road bike inner tube over the frame. Insert the pin through the tube to the mark and tie-wrap the tube to secure it.

Sealing the headset

Place a cover over the headset to provide protection. You can fit a protector to the headset without removing any components by simply joining up the velcro.

Fitting mudguards

Fasten a mudguard to the seat pin and you will block much of the spray from the back wheel. For the front wheel, fit a guard that clips on to the frame and is secured in place with tie-wraps. Full mudguards, which attach to the fork and rear drop-out, give almost full protection for on-road biking but get clogged up off-road.

Weatherproofing the transmission

Cleaning and lubricating the chain

Lubricate and clean your chain as often as you do in summer and after every wet ride. Apply the same light lubricant that you use in the summer and then apply a heavier oil, which will not wash off as easily. Only coat the rollers and insides of each link with heavier oil because it attracts more dirt.

Cleaning and lubricating mechs

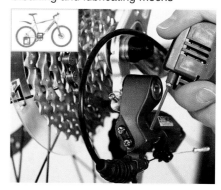

Dribble oil on to the pivots around which the front and rear mechs move. Use a heavier, wet oil rather than the oil you would normally apply during the summer. Every time you dribble oil like this, first flush out the old oil by dribbling some degreaser on to the pivots and letting it sink in for a few minutes.

Cleaning and lubricating pedals

Apply heavier, wet oil to lubricate the retention mechanism of clipless pedals after degreasing all the moving parts. The heavier oil will not wash off as easily as dry oil. Regularly clean off old oil with degreaser and apply new oil in order to prevent the accumulation of grit and the consequent increase in pedal wear.

3

MAINTAINING YOUR

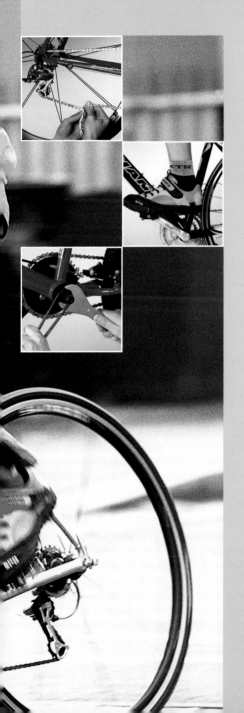

The transmission is the heart of your bike. Fine-tune and regularly service the system to ensure that the gear-shifters, chain, chainset, cassette, and mechs work together in perfect harmony.

TRANSMISSION

CABLES AND SHIFTERS

Cables and shifters enable the rider to operate the gears. Cables are under constant tension and need to be replaced regularly and kept well lubricated. They must also be inspected often and replaced if they show signs of wear. Shifters require only occasional lubrication of their inner workings.

How they work

An inner cable connects the gear-shifter to the mech, and allows the rider to change gear. Gear-shifts made by a gear shifter cause the front mech to shift the chain from one chainring to another, or the rear mech to shift the chain from one sprocket to another. Pulling the gear cable shifts the chain from a smaller to a larger chainring or sprocket; releasing the gear cable shifts the chain from a larger to a smaller chainring or sprocket. The left-hand shifter controls the front mech; the right-hand shifter controls the rear mech.

Controlling the gears
The cables and shifters on a bike allow the rider to effortlessly control the gear system.

Cable clamp
Attaches the cable to the rear mech

Rear mech
Moves the chain from one sprocket to another

REAR MECH CABLE

A clamp connects the cable to the rear mech. When the shifter is pushed, the cable pulls the rear mech inwards, moving the chain from a smaller to a larger sprocket. When the shifter releases the cable tension, the springs on the rear mech pull the jockey wheels, and the chain, back to a smaller sprocket.

Front mech
Moves the chain from one chainring to another

SHIFTING GEAR

In this Campagnolo shifter, the rider pushes the inner shift lever to pull the cable and move the mech. When the rider depresses a lever on the inner side of the lever hood, the cable is released and the mech moves back.

Gear-shifter
Pulls and releases the rear mech

COMBINED BRAKE LEVER/GEAR SHIFTER ANATOMY

Gear-shifters are often combined with the brake levers on the handlebar. On this Shimano gear-shifter, the brake lever also acts as a shift lever. When the rider pushes the brake lever inwards with the fingers, the control cable attached to it is pulled and a ratchet mechanism is lifted. A click of this mechanism equals one shift of the front or rear mech, which moves the chain across the chainring or sprockets. The ratchet mechanism then holds the cable in its new position. When the rider pushes the inner shift lever inwards, the ratchet mechanism's hold is released and so the shifter's pull on the cable ceases.

Cable
Connects the shifter to the rear mech

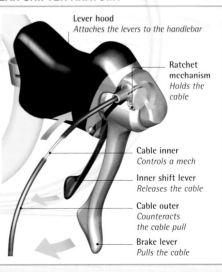

Lever hood
Attaches the levers to the handlebar

Ratchet mechanism
Holds the cable

Cable inner
Controls a mech

Inner shift lever
Releases the cable

Cable outer
Counteracts the cable pull

Brake lever
Pulls the cable

Drop handlebar gear cables

Keeping gear cables clean and lubricated, and replacing them if they fray, is very important for smooth shifting. Change them as a matter of course at least once a year, or more often if you are a heavy user.

Lubrication reduces the effects of friction between the inner cable and the cable outer, and helps to keep out water and grit. If the gears become difficult to shift to a different chainring or sprocket, the cable is probably dry and needs lubrication.

Friction increases with cable length. Cut cable outers as short as possible, but not so short that they constrict the cable or restrict the steering. If you are unsure how much cable outer to cut, look at the arc of the outers on other bikes (see pp. 10–17).

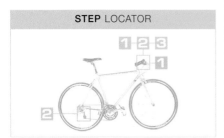

STEP LOCATOR

Parts of gear-shift units

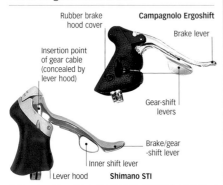

Rubber brake hood cover

Campagnolo Ergoshift

Brake lever

Insertion point of gear cable (concealed by lever hood)

Gear-shift levers

Brake/gear -shift lever

Inner shift lever

Lever hood   **Shimano STI**

Toolbox

- Allen key multi-tool • Long-nosed pliers
- Cable cutters

Replacing a Shimano gear cable

1 **Place the gear-shifter** in the smallest sprocket for the rear shifter and the smallest chainring position for the front shifter.

- Pull back the brake lever and remove the old cable from a hole on the outer side of the lever.
- Insert a new lubricated cable into the hole.
- Ease the cable through the hole and insert it into the cable outer.

Replacing a Campagnolo gear cable

1 **Remove the handlebar tape** as the cable outer runs underneath it. You also need to do this if you are replacing a brake cable.

- Carefully unwind the old tape from the centre of the handlebar to just below the shifter and leave it hanging while you carry out the work.
- Pull the rubber brake hood cover forwards to free the tape beneath it. Pull the tape off slowly.

2 **Pull the gear cable** through pre-cut lengths of cable outer with the long-nosed pliers.

• For the rear mech, this requires one length from the shifter to the cable guide on the down tube, and another length from the guide on the right-hand chainstay to the rear mech's barrel adjuster.

• Place metal ferrules on the cut end of each outer so that it fits snugly into the cable guide.

• Finally, pull the cable through the barrel adjuster and cable-clamp bolt. Then tighten the bolt with the Allen key.

2 **Put the rear shifter** in the smallest sprocket and the front shifter in the smallest chainring. Remove the old cable from under the hood cover.

• Grease the new cable and push it through the hole under the hood cover.

3 **Dribble oil into a cable outer,** which should be cut to fit between the cable guide and the component. If it is cut too short, it constricts; if it is too long, it increases friction (see pp.26–7).

• Ensure that metal ferrules are placed on the ends of all the cable outers on your bike.

• Insert the cable into the cable outer. Keep the cable to the mech under tension as you clamp it.

Straight handlebar gear cables

Looking after and replacing the gear cables on a mountain bike is very similar to a road bike. However, mountain bikes are often subjected to harsher conditions than road bikes so the cables must be replaced and lubricated more regularly.

Take special care with the cable disc brakes of a mountain bike because they have longer lengths of cable outer and the cables require lubricating more often.

Rear gear cables can slap against the frame when you ride a mountain bike over rough ground. If this happens regularly, it may mark the paintwork so try fitting tiny rubber rings over the exposed cable to protect the frame.

STEP LOCATOR

Parts of gear-shift units

Barrel adjuster | **SRAM Grip Shift**
Shifter body
Gear indicator
Cable port
Ring clamp
Shimano Rapidfire
Gear-shift levers
Barrel adjuster

Toolbox
- 5mm Allen key • Long-nosed pliers
- Cable cutters • Cable pullers

Replacing a Rapidfire gear cable

1 **Remove the old cable** with long-nosed pliers and put the shifter in the smallest sprocket or chainring position.

● Insert the end of the new, lubricated cable into the hole where the cable nipple sits inside the shifter.

● Check the route of your existing cable and follow the route when fitting a new cable in Step 4.

3 **Cut both the cable and cable outers** with your cable cutters to the same length as the old ones you have removed. Make the outers long enough to allow the cable to travel freely inside.

● Dribble a drop of oil down each cable outer.

● Fit a ferrule to the end of each cable outer to ensure that it fits tightly into the frame's cable guides (see pp.26–7).

Replacing a Grip Shift gear cable

Push the cable into the hole until its end shows through the barrel adjuster on the outside of the shifter body.

● Thread the cable through the first length of lubricated cable outer.

Put the rear shifter into the smallest sprocket and the front shifter into the smallest chainring.

● Lift the cable port to reveal the old cable and remove it with long-nosed pliers.

● Spray a small amount of light oil into the mechanism while the port is off.

Thread the inner cable through each length of outer cable.

● For a rear mech, unscrew the barrel adjuster to about half its range and insert the inner cable. For a front mech, insert the cable into the clamp.

● Pull hard with your cable pullers and tighten the cable clamp. Cut off any excess cable.

Grease the new cable, insert it into the Grip Shift, and push it until the end protrudes from the other side of the shifter.

● Thread the cable through each outer and secure to either the front or rear mech as in Step 4 for Replacing a Rapidfire gear cable (*left*).

● Replace the cable port, cut off any excess, and fit a cable tidy to the cable end (*see pp.26–7*).

FRONT AND REAR MECHS

The two mechs move the chain smoothly between the sprockets and chainrings, but only if the travel of the mechs is set up correctly. The mech pivots and jockey wheels must be checked for wear and lubricated. The front mech must be properly aligned with the chainrings.

How they work

The front and rear mechs change the gears on a bike. To change up a gear, the shifter is used to pull on the cable, which causes the front mech to push the chain from a smaller to a larger chainring or the rear mech to push the chain from a smaller to a larger sprocket. To change down a gear, the cable is released, causing the springs in both mechs to move the chain to a smaller chainring or sprocket. Each mech moves around a pivot point. High and low adjusting screws ensure that the mechs do not push the chain beyond the largest chainring or sprocket, or pull it beyond the smallest. This range is called the mech's travel. Once its travel is set up, and provided the cable tension is sufficient, the mech will make a single, clean gear-shift for every click of the shifter.

Rear mech
Transfers the chain from one sprocket to another

Cable
Pushes and pulls the rear mech

REAR MECH ANATOMY

To change gear, two jockey wheels transfer the chain on to a different sprocket. They move in the same plane as the chain and are spring-loaded to preserve the tension in the chain. Two mech plates enable the jockey wheels to change gear upwards, while the plate spring enables the jockey wheels to change gear downwards.

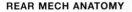

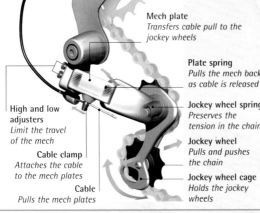

Mech plate
Transfers cable pull to the jockey wheels

Plate spring
Pulls the mech back as cable is released

High and low adjusters
Limit the travel of the mech

Jockey wheel spring
Preserves the tension in the chain

Cable clamp
Attaches the cable to the mech plates

Jockey wheel
Pulls and pushes the chain

Cable
Pulls the mech plates

Jockey wheel cage
Holds the jockey wheels

Working with the shifters
The front and rear mechs work in harmony with the shifters to provide easy, quick, and accurate gear-shifts whenever the rider needs them.

REAR MECH IN USE

When the cable is pulled, it causes both the mech plates to swing inwards on four pivot points, causing the jockey wheels to guide the chain on to a larger sprocket. When the cable is released, the plate spring moves the chain back to a smaller sprocket.

Large sprocket *The chain is moved to the largest sprocket by the pull of the cable.*

Small sprocket *The chain is returned to the smallest sprocket by the plate spring.*

FRONT MECH ANATOMY

When pulled, the cable moves the outer arm, which acts like a lever on a pivot point to push the front mech cage away from the bike. This moves the chain from a smaller to a larger chainring. When the cable is released, a spring on the mech's inner arm pulls the cage back towards the bike.

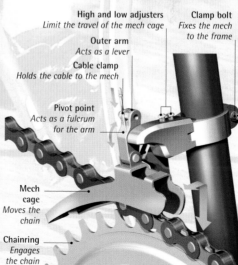

High and low adjusters *Limit the travel of the mech cage*

Clamp bolt *Fixes the mech to the frame*

Outer arm *Acts as a lever*

Cable clamp *Holds the cable to the mech*

Pivot point *Acts as a fulcrum for the arm*

Mech cage *Moves the chain*

Chainring *Engages the chain*

Front mech *Transfers the chain from one chainring to another*

Chainring *Carries the chain*

Front mech

Front mechs (short for "mechanism") shift the chain from one chainring to the next. There are two main kinds: braze-on mechs (*below*) are fixed by an Allen bolt to a lug, or protrusion, on the bike frame; band-on mechs are attached to a band that goes around the frame and is part of the mech.

There are two important maintenance jobs for a front mech: setting it up after fitting a new control cable and adjusting it when it is not shifting properly. You should also clean the mech regularly to prevent the build-up of dirt, which interferes with the way it works and will quickly wear it out.

For the mech to work perfectly, the lower edge of the mech cage's outer side should be no higher than 2mm above the largest chainring. The cage's outer side must also be parallel with the chainrings.

Correct shifts depend on the front mech travelling a certain distance per shift. High and low adjusting screws on the mech will control this travel.

STEP LOCATOR

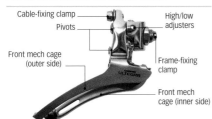

Parts of a braze-on front mech

Cable-fixing clamp — Pivots — Front mech cage (outer side) — High/low adjusters — Frame-fixing clamp — Front mech cage (inner side)

Toolbox
- Long-nosed pliers ● 5mm Allen key
- Screwdriver ● Cable cutters

Adjusting a front mech

1 **Shift the chain** into the largest sprocket and the smallest chainring.

● Pull the front mech cage away from the frame. Note the distance by which the lower edge of its outer side clears the largest chainring. This should be 2mm. If it is more or less, undo the frame-fixing clamp and raise or lower the front mech.

● Line up the cage parallel with the chainrings and tighten the frame-fixing clamp.

3 **Pull the gear cable** through the cable clamp and tighten the cable-clamp bolt.

● Cut off any excess cable with your cable cutters and crimp on a cable tidy (*see pp.26–7*).

● Repeat Steps 2 and 3 if, after a couple of rides, the chain will not shift up to the next chainring, since cables can sometimes stretch slightly.

2 **Undo the cable-fixing clamp** until the cable becomes free.

● Look for the low gear adjuster (usually marked "L") and screw it in or out until the inner side of the front mech cage is about 2mm from the chain. You have now set the starting point of the mech's travel.

● Take this opportunity to clean the guide in which the cable runs under the bottom-bracket shell. Use degreaser, and then wash and dry the whole area.

● Put a little dry lubricant in the guide.

4 **Shift the chain** across until it is in the smallest sprocket and the largest chainring.

● Repeat Steps 2 and 3 if the chain will not shift on to the largest chainring.

5 **Screw in the high adjuster** (usually marked "H") to bring the outer side of the front mech cage to about 2mm from the chain.

● Unscrew the higher adjuster to allow more travel if, when you shift on to the largest chainring, the chain does not move on to it.

● Check the action by shifting a few times between all the chainrings.

Rear mech

Most rear mechs are indexed, which means that for every click of the shifter, either up or down, the mech will shift the chain from one sprocket to the next.

Occasionally, you may find that the chain does not quite move on to the next sprocket when you make a single shift, or else it skips a sprocket in an overshift. In either case, the rear mech needs adjusting. You will also need to follow the steps in this sequence whenever you fit a new cable (see pp.46–9).

To ensure that the rear mech works faultlessly, pay particular attention to its jockey wheels because this is where oil and dirt can accumulate. Degrease and scrub them every time you clean your bike (see pp.28–9). Whenever you lubricate the jockey wheels or the rear mech pivots, make sure that you wipe off any excess oil.

STEP LOCATOR

Parts of a rear mech

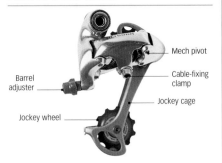

Mech pivot

Barrel adjuster

Cable-fixing clamp

Jockey cage

Jockey wheel

Toolbox

- Long-nosed pliers • Cable cutters
- 5mm Allen key • Screwdriver

Adjusting a rear mech

1 **Shift the chain** on to the biggest chainring and smallest sprocket, then undo the cable-fixing clamp so that the cable hangs free.

- Check the cable and fit a new one if it shows any sign of fraying (see p.39).

- Screw the barrel adjuster in or out, until it is at half of its range.

4 **Shift back to the smallest sprocket,** then shift upwards through each gear. If the rear mech does not shift all the way on to the next biggest sprocket, screw out the barrel adjuster until it does. If the mech over-shifts and skips a sprocket, screw in the barrel adjuster until it stops.

2 **Use the high adjuster** (usually marked "H") to line up the jockey wheels with the smallest sprocket.

● Once you have lined them up, rotate the pedals forwards while adjusting the "H" adjuster until the chain runs smoothly.

● Pull the cable downwards through the cable-fixing clamp and re-clamp it.

3 **Shift on to the smallest chainring** and largest sprocket.

● Push the rear mech with your fingers towards the spokes. If it moves beyond the largest sprocket, screw in the low adjuster (marked "L") until the mech stops at the largest sprocket.

● Turn the pedals to see if the chain runs smoothly. If it does not, adjust the "L" in or out.

5 **Prevent the jockey wheels** from making contact with the bigger sprockets by screwing in the adjuster that butts on to the rear mech hanger on the frame drop-out. Remember to make this adjustment if you fit a block or cassette with bigger sprockets than usual.

HUB GEARS

Hub gears located inside the hub casing alter the speed at which the back wheel revolves. They require little routine maintenance and, since they are sealed, most hub-gear systems do not need to be lubricated regularly. The control cables must still be inspected regularly and replaced if they are worn.

How they work

All hub gears work according to the same basic principle. A system of internal cogs make the hub casing, and therefore the rear wheel, turn at a different speed to a single, external sprocket that is driven by the pedals via the chain. The sprocket is connected to the cogs by a driver unit and the cogs rotate the hub casing at different speeds. Spokes attach the casing to the rim, thereby revolving the rear wheel.

A shifter on the handlebar operates a mechanism attached to the hub. This mechanism causes various combinations of different-sized cogs within the hub to engage with a ring gear, which drives the hub casing. Each combination gives a different gear ratio, and the number of gears depends on the number of cogs within the hub.

SHIMANO NEXUS HUB GEAR ANATOMY

To change gear, the rider activates the shifter to pull the cable, which turns the satellite on the drive side of the hub. This triggers a mechanism within the driver unit to move two carrier units containing cogs. Different cogs are brought into contact with the ring gears. When the cable is released, the spring-loaded carrier units move the cogs back to a different combination.

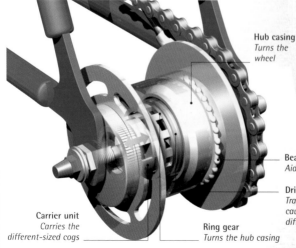

Cable and satellite
Side view of the hub

Hub casing
Turns the wheel

Bearings
Aid the rotation of the hub casing

Driver unit
Transfers the sprocket's drive and causes the carrier unit to engage different cogs with the ring gear

Carrier unit
Carries the different-sized cogs

Ring gear
Turns the hub casing

Protecting the gears
The hub gear mechanism is fully enclosed to protect it from damage, dirt, and water.

Hub gear unit
Contains the cogs that allow gear changes

Hub gear I

If the cable to your hub gear breaks or frays, you will need to replace it. Before making a start, first identify the hub gear units on your bike from the manufacturer's name. This is usually stamped on the hub and the number of gears is indicated on the shifter.

The hub-gear model illustrated in the steps of this sequence is the Shimano Nexus 7-speed gear, which is operated by a twist grip shifter. Alternatively, bikes may be equipped with SRAM hub gears, as well as those made by other manufacturers, that are operated by thumbshifters.

Some older bikes have Sturmey Archer 3-speed gears. Although they all work on the same principle, the methods used to change a cable are subtly different. Try to find the manufacturer's instructions for the gear fitted to your bike – ask at bike shops or search the internet.

STEP LOCATOR

Parts of a hub gear

Seat for cable-retaining bolt

Right-hand axle nut

Lockring

Cable route

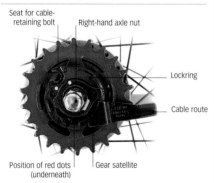

Position of red dots (underneath)

Gear satellite

Toolbox

● Spanners to fit wheel axle nuts and cable-clamp bolt ● Flat-bladed screwdriver

Replacing a hub-gear cable

1 **Put the shifter into first gear.** At this point, there is no tension on the cable, so it is the starting point for fitting a new cable. If the cable is broken, the hub gear will have automatically returned to first gear, so move the shifter there to line up the system.

4 **Insert the cable** through the chainstay cable guide and make sure that the outer is well-seated into the guide.

● Pull the cable tight and tighten the clamp bolt on to it at exactly the distance you measured from the cable guide in Step 2.

● Now push the clamp bolt back into the place where it sits on the gear satellite (*inset*).

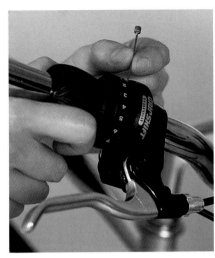

2 **Remove the rear wheel** (see *pp.136–37*) and push the wheel forwards out of the drop-out.

● Use a flat screwdriver to lever out the cable-clamp bolt from the position in which it sits on the gear satellite.

● Pull on the clamp bolt and measure the length of the cable between it and the chainstay cable guide. Undo the clamp to remove it from the old cable.

3 **Remove the cable port** on the plastic part of the shifter, where the pointer indicates which gear the system is in.

● Take the old cable out of the shifter by pushing it from behind, or pull it out by its nipple.

● Insert the greased new cable into the shifter. Dribble a little oil inside the outer and then push the new cable through the outer.

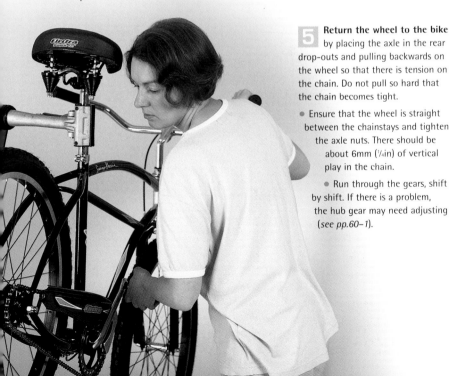

5 **Return the wheel to the bike** by placing the axle in the rear drop-outs and pulling backwards on the wheel so that there is tension on the chain. Do not pull so hard that the chain becomes tight.

● Ensure that the wheel is straight between the chainstays and tighten the axle nuts. There should be about 6mm (¼in) of vertical play in the chain.

● Run through the gears, shift by shift. If there is a problem, the hub gear may need adjusting (see *pp.60–1*).

Hub gear II

Occasionally, you might be unable to engage a particular gear because dirt has interfered with the gear satellite's action. You will need to remove the satellite to clean it and this means removing the rear wheel.

On other occasions, you might find that the shift has lost some of its smoothness. In this case, the cable has probably stretched so that the shifter is out of phase with the gear mechanism. To remedy this problem, use the barrel adjuster on the shifter to take up any slack in the cable.

Every time the wheel is removed and put back on to your bike, run through the gears and check that they are shifting correctly. If they are not, follow the last two steps of this sequence in order to make sure that the gears are running smoothly.

Finally, the hub-gear system has clear markings – look for the red dots and the yellow dots and triangles – to help you to set up the gears.

If a bike is fitted with a Sturmey Archer 3-speed hub gear, it may occasionally shift to second gear, but without any drive. When this happens, put the shifter into the third gear position and look at the cable where it runs along the chainstay. The cable will be slack so that it sags. Undo the cable-clamp bolt near to the hub-gear unit and pull the cable through the clamp until it runs in a straight line. Re-clamp the bolt and the gears will shift perfectly.

STEP LOCATOR

Toolbox

- Spanners to fit wheel axle nuts

Adjusting your hub-gear assembly

1 **Remove the rear wheel** by undoing and removing both its axle bolts (*see pp.136–37*). The satellite is locked on to the hub by a lockring. Turn the lockring by hand until its yellow dot lines up with the one on the satellite.

- Lift off the lockring to free the satellite.

3 **Put the satellite back** on to the wheel. Line up its triangles with those on the axle.

- Press the satellite home on to the hub.

- Replace the lockring, pushing it on to the satellite so that its yellow dot lines up with the yellow dot on the satellite.

- Turn the lockring so that the dots are separated. The satellite is now locked in place.

2 Lift the satellite from the hub body, noting the relative positions of the two yellow triangles that are marked on it.

● Note the position of two more yellow triangles on the bare axle that is left inside the wheel.

● Flush out the freed gear satellite with degreaser. Let this drain out and spray light oil into the satellite.

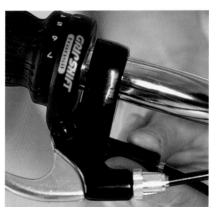

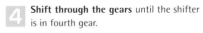

4 Shift through the gears until the shifter is in fourth gear.

● Use the barrel adjuster on the shifter to fine-tune the gear adjustment. Tilt the bike so that you can see the underside of the hub gear.

5 Look for the two red dots on the gear mechanism. One is marked on the satellite and one on the lockring. Both dots are marked on the underside of the gear where the cable runs. In fourth gear, these two dots should line up. If they do not, screw the barrel adjuster in or out until the dots line up. When they do line up, all the gear-shifts will be perfect.

CHAIN, CASSETTE, AND CHAINSET

With every turn of the pedals the chain, cassette, and chainset are put under strain. The parts are in continual contact, and the motion of pedalling inevitably leads to wear. No matter how well you look after each part, they will eventually need removing and replacing.

How they work

The chain, cassette, and chainset combine to form the heart of the transmission, the part of the bike through which a rider's pedal power is transferred into forward motion. The pedals drive the chainset and, via the chain, turn a sprocket attached to the hub of the rear wheel, which in turn rotates the wheel.

Bikes with derailleur gears use mechs to shift the chain on to different-sized sprockets and chainrings, which make up the cassette and chainset. Each combination of chainring and sprocket provides a different gear ratio, giving up to 27 different gears that can be used to tackle anything from steep climbs to gentle flats.

Chain
Feeds through jockey wheels

Rear mech
Shifts the chain across the sprocke[r]

Sprockets
Driven by the chain

EXPLODED CASSETTE

The cassette transfers the motion of the chain to the wheel. It consists of sprockets that slide on to the cassette body, which is bolted on to the hub. The cassette body houses the freewheel, which allows the wheel to turn when the cassette is stationary.

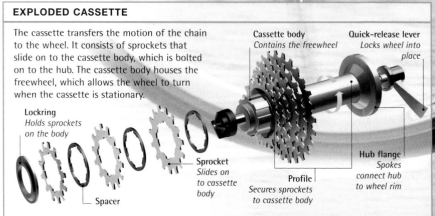

Cassette body
Contains the freewheel

Quick-release lever
Locks wheel into place

Lockring
Holds sprockets on the body

Sprocket
Slides on to cassette body

Profile
Secures sprockets to cassette body

Hub flange
Spokes connect hub to wheel rim

Spacer

CHAIN ANATOMY

The chain is the key to transmitting pedal power into forward motion.

To transfer power efficiently the chain must be strong, but flexible enough to fit securely around the teeth of the chainrings and sprockets. To achieve this, a series of links articulate around joining pins, which are surrounded by revolving metal barrels.

Joining pin
Connects inner and outer links

Barrel
Sits between teeth of chainrings and sprockets

Outer link
Shaped to allow quick gear shifts

Inner link
Rotates around the barrel

Rear wheel
Driven by the sprockets

Chainset
Powered by pedalling

Chainring
Carries the chain around the chainset

Chain
Transmits power from the chainset

Pedal
Transmits energy to the chainset

Lightweight components
The chain, cassette, and chainset are lightweight items that use the latest design and construction techniques to maximize strength and durability while maintaining an aerodynamic profile.

Chains

Replacing a chain is a regular maintenance task. All chains eventually wear out, even if you clean and lubricate them properly. A worn chain, as well as being inefficient, will quickly wear out other transmission parts, and so prove expensive.

To determine how much a chain has become worn, either use a specialist gauge from a bike shop or measure the length of 24 links. If the length is greater than 300mm (12in), the chain is worn.

New chains on derailleur gear systems are linked with a joining pin that comes with the chain. You will need a link extractor tool to make this join. The thicker chains of hub gears, BMX bikes, and some fixed-gear bikes are joined by split links.

STEP LOCATOR

Parts of a split-link and a Shimano chain

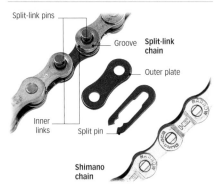

Split-link pins

Groove — **Split-link chain**

Outer plate

Inner links

Split pin

Shimano chain

Toolbox
- Chain link extractor
- Long-nosed pliers

Replacing a derailleur chain

1 **Shift on to the smallest chainring** and sprocket so that the chain is slack.

- Place a link in the link extractor and push out the pin until the chain breaks.
- Remove the old chain with the link extractor.

3 **Remove the excess links** from the opposite end to the one on which there is a joining link. Leave an inner link so that the two ends can be joined together.

- Join the chain by pushing the pin of the joining link through the opposite inner link with the extractor tool.

Joining a split-link chain

2 **Thread a new chain** through the jockey wheels and around the biggest chainring and smallest sprocket.

● Pull the ends of the chain together so that there is a little tension in the jockey wheels. This establishes the length of chain you need.

1 **Join the chain** by pressing the side of the split link with the pins fixed in its plate through the two inner-link ends of the chain.

● Press the other plate on to the pins that are now sticking through the inner links.

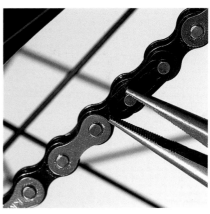

4 **Loosen any stiff links** that occur when the chain links are compressed during Step 3.

● Flex the stiff links with a little sideways pressure until they become loose (*inset*).

● Remove the protruding part of the pin after joining a Shimano chain, as these have an extra-long joining pin.

● Break off the excess with long-nosed pliers.

2 **Push the split pin** into the grooves of the split-link pins. These are sticking through the outer plate that you have just fitted. The split pin's open end should face the rear of the bike.

● Fix the split pin in place by pushing it home with long-nosed pliers until you feel it click.

Cassette and freewheel

The cassette and freewheel allow the rear wheel to rotate while the pedals remain stationary. Their internal mechanisms – the freehub body of a cassette and the block in a freewheel – will eventually wear out and need replacing. The sprockets on both can also wear. These parts will also need to be removed whenever you replace a broken spoke on the drive side of the rear wheel.

The tools for removing a freewheel and a cassette depend on the manufacturer of the part that is fitted to the bike. Usually, the manufacturer's name is stamped on the component. However, if you are in any doubt about which tool you need, take the wheel to the shop when buying a remover tool.

STEP LOCATOR

Parts of a freewheel and a cassette

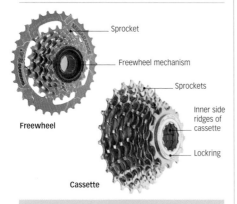

Sprocket

Freewheel mechanism

Sprockets

Inner side ridges of cassette

Lockring

Freewheel

Cassette

Toolbox
- Spanners ● Cassette remover ● Chain whip
- Block remover ● Grease

Removing a cassette

1 **Remove the quick-release skewer** from the rear wheel.

● Insert the cassette remover into the teeth of the lockring at the centre of the cassette.

● Replace the quick-release skewer to secure the cassette remover.

Removing a freewheel block

1 **Remove the quick-release skewer** and insert the block remover into the teeth at the block's centre.

● Lock the block remover in place by replacing the quick-release skewer.

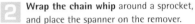 **Wrap the chain whip** around a sprocket, and place the spanner on the remover.

- Press downwards on both tools. This holds the cassette, while the remover unlocks the lockring.

- Remove the quick-release skewer once the lockring starts turning.

- Continue to unscrew the lockring with the cassette remover.

Take off the smallest sprocket after you have removed the lockring. On many cassettes, the remaining sprockets come off in one piece. If they do not, you must put individual sprockets back in a certain way. Failure to do so will affect the precision of gear shifts. Usually, the sprockets are marked, so that lining up these marks ensures the correct sprocket orientation.

Put the spanner on the flats of the block remover and turn anticlockwise.

- As the block begins to move, remove the quick-release skewer and continue turning until the block comes off.

Check the integral freewheel mechanism, which is independent of the hub. Replace it with a new block if it is worn.

- Coat the threads of the hub with grease, then screw the block on by hand.

- Lock the block in place by tightening it with the spanner and the block remover.

Chainsets

Removing a chainset is a useful skill to have because it will allow you to replace an old crank, clean or replace a worn chainring, or work on the bottom bracket.

Some chainsets are held in place by a hexagonal bolt, which can be removed with a chainset socket spanner (*see Step 1*). Other chainsets are equipped with self-removing Allen bolts, which can be detached with an 8mm Allen key (*see Step 2*).

When refitting a chainset, keep grease or oil from touching the axle. The chainset must be dry when fitted to the axle or it will work loose. After refitting, go for a short ride and then try the axle bolt again. If it is slightly loose, you should tighten it.

Step 5 shows how to remove a chainring so that you can replace one that is worn or fit a bigger or smaller chainring that will provide you with different gear ratios.

STEP LOCATOR

Parts of a chainset

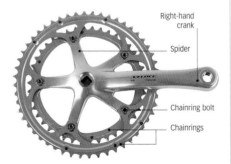

Right-hand crank

Spider

Chainring bolt

Chainrings

Toolbox

- Crank extractor • 5mm Allen key
- 8mm Allen key or chainset socket spanner
- Chainring bolt peg spanner

Removing a chainset

1 **Detach a hexagonal chainset bolt** from the axle with a chainset socket spanner. Normal socket spanners are often too thick to fit into the space where the bolt is located.

- Steady the crank with your free hand to give you something to push against. Work from below the chainset so that if your hand or the spanner slips, the chainring teeth will not injure you.

- To remove the chainset, go to Step 4.

4 **Use a crank extractor** to remove the chainset if it is not the self-removing type. Make sure that the washer beneath the bolt has also been removed.

- Carefully screw the extractor into the delicate threads at the centre of the chainset. When the extractor is fully in, turn its handle clockwise to pull off the chainset.

2 **Unscrew a self-removing Allen bolt** with an 8mm Allen key. These kinds of bolt extract the chainset as you unscrew them.

● Steady the crank with your free hand to give you something to push against. Work from below the chainset so that if your hand or the spanner slips, the chainring teeth will not injure you.

● To remove the chainring, go to Step 5.

3 **Use a long-handled Allen key** if there is an Allen bolt holding the chainset on your bike. Usually, an 8mm key is the size required.

● Work from below the chainset so that if you slip the chainring teeth will not injure you.

● To remove the chainset, go to Step 4.

5 **Remove the chainring** with a 5mm Allen key on one side and a chainring bolt peg spanner to hold the bolt on the other. You can do this without taking the chainset off the axle, but you must remove it if you are working on the inner rings of some triple chainsets.

● Cure a creaking noise from the chainset by putting grease on the threads of the chainring bolts before you reassemble the chainset. Standard chainring bolts are made from steel. Be especially careful not to over-tighten aluminium or titanium bolts.

BOTTOM BRACKETS

There are two main types of bottom bracket: open-bearing bottom brackets, which are exposed to water and grit, and must be regularly inspected for signs of wear and damage; and cartridge-bearing bottom brackets, which are usually sealed from the elements.

How they work

The bottom bracket joins the crank of each pedal with an axle, which rotates in the bike's frame. Each type of bracket consists of an axle, two bearings, two threaded cups (the free cup and fixed cup), and, in some types, a sleeve. The axle rotates freely on the bearings, which are held at one end of the axle within the free cup and at the other, drive-side end, by the fixed cup. The cranks are screwed into the internal threading of the axle. The axle of a third type of bottom bracket, the BMX bracket, is threaded externally – the whole bracket is held in place by a locknut that screws on to this thread on the left-hand crank side of the axle.

Providing strength
The axle and bearings of the bottom bracket need to be both strong and reliable enough to bear the weight and power of the rider.

CARTRIDGE-BEARING BOTTOM BRACKET ANATOMY

Each of the cartridge bearings is composed of ball-bearings, which are sandwiched between an inner and outer race by plastic seals. The cartridge bearings are located close to each end of the bottom-bracket axle. A tubular sleeve fits over the two bearings, filling the space between them. The fixed and free cups fit over this sleeve to create a totally sealed unit.

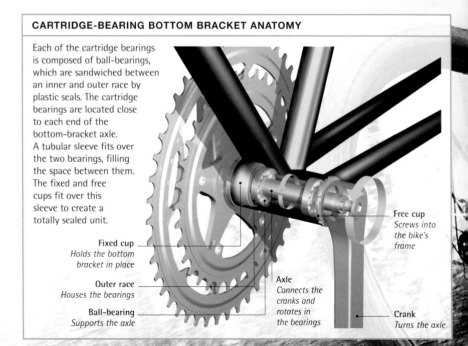

Fixed cup
Holds the bottom bracket in place

Outer race
Houses the bearings

Ball-bearing
Supports the axle

Axle
Connects the cranks and rotates in the bearings

Free cup
Screws into the bike's frame

Crank
Turns the axle

OPEN-BEARING BOTTOM BRACKET ANATOMY

The axle of an open-bearing bottom bracket rotates on ball-bearings set in a cage that butts up against a raised bearing surface. The cups hold the axle/bearing assembly in place. The fixed cup screws all the way into the frame. The free cup screws in until the axle is held without play, but still rotates freely. A lockring holds the free cup in place.

Axle
Connects the cranks and rotates in the bearings

Lockring
Fixes the bottom bracket in position

Ball-bearing
Lets the axle turn

Free cup
Screws into the bike's frame

Crank
Turns the axle

Fixed cup
Holds the bottom bracket in place

Bearing surface
Ensures that the axle rotates smoothly on the bearings

Crank
Turns the axle

Cartridge-bearing bottom bracket
Allows the smooth rotation of the axle

Cartridge bottom bracket

Cartridge bottom brackets require no routine maintenance. Their bearings are sealed from the elements – even from the water you use for hosing or pressure-washing your bike, provided that you turn the pedals forwards during the wash.

When the bearings do eventually wear out you will have to replace the whole unit. The remover tools for this job are specific to each particular bottom bracket, so check which make is fitted to your bike before buying the tools.

If you are planning a replacement, there are three types of bottom bracket axle to choose: square-tapered, Shimano Octalink, and Isis. The type used in the steps in this sequence is square-tapered; the type shown below is Octalink. Finally, if your bike is fitted with an Italian-threaded bottom bracket, marked 36 x 1, ask a bike shop to help with replacing it.

STEP LOCATOR

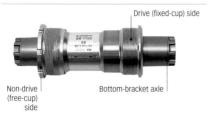

Parts of a cartridge bottom bracket

Drive (fixed-cup) side

Non-drive (free-cup) side

Bottom-bracket axle

Toolbox

- Measuring callipers • Ruler • Spanner
- Cartridge bottom bracket remover • Grease

Installing a cartridge bottom bracket

1 **Put the bike on a workstand** and remove the chainset (see pp.68–9).

● Use a pair of callipers to measure the length of the old axle before you remove the bottom bracket, so that you can be sure the replacement has an axle of the same length. You need to do this because different chainsets are designed to work with different axle lengths.

4 **Grease the threads** of each side of the new bottom bracket for easier fitting. The non-drive threads are sometimes referred to as the free-cup and the drive-side threads are known as the fixed cup. Do not grease the drive side of a bottom bracket with Italian threads.

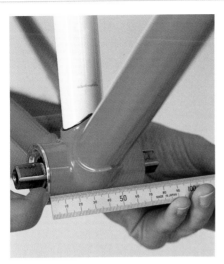

2 **Measure the width** of the bottom-bracket shell with a ruler. The shell forms part of the bike's frame and will be either 68mm (2³⁄₄in) or 73mm (3in) wide. This width determines the width of the bracket unit you need to buy.

3 **Remove both the cranks** (see pp.68–9), insert a bottom-bracket remover into the non-drive side of the bracket and turn the remover anticlockwise with a spanner.

● Repeat on the other side, turning clockwise. Turn it anticlockwise if your bike has an Italian-threaded bottom bracket (marked 36 x 1).

5 **Insert the bottom bracket** from the drive (fixed-cup) side using the remover tool. Fit the teeth of the tool into the indentations of the bottom bracket (see enlargement).

● Insert the non-drive (free-cup) side when the drive side is almost in position. Use the remover to screw it in a few turns. Fully tighten the drive side, then the non-drive side.

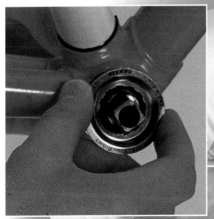

Open-bearing bottom bracket

Many older bikes are fitted with an open-bearing bottom bracket. To test the bracket for wear, take the chain off the chainrings and turn the chainset by hand in a pedalling action. If you hear grinding noises, or if the action feels rough, check the bracket. Then hold one of the cranks near the pedal and push it inwards – more than 1mm of play means the bracket needs servicing.

The bearings may suffer more wear than those in cartridge-bearing brackets because they are not as well sealed and so let in dirt and water. However, regular cleaning and lubrication can drastically reduce this wear. A properly adjusted open-bearing bottom bracket is subject to less internal friction than many cartridge-bearing brackets.

If a bottom-bracket cup proves difficult to remove or refit, ask any good bike shop for help – they will have specialist removal equipment and tools to clean and reinstate the shell threads.

STEP LOCATOR

Parts of an open-bearing bottom bracket

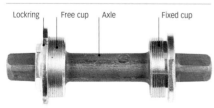

Lockring | Free cup | Axle | Fixed cup

Toolbox

- C-spanner • Peg spanner
- Fixed-cup spanner

Maintaining an open-bearing bottom bracket

1 First remove both the cranks (*see Steps 1–4, pp.68–9*).

● Use a C-spanner to remove the lockring on the non-drive (free-cup) side. Turn the C-spanner anticlockwise for all bikes.

● Make sure that the hook of the C-spanner is correctly located in one of the notches around the lockring. You need to use a fair amount of force, so be careful.

3 Remove the fixed cup on the drive side of the bike by using a fixed-cup spanner on its two flats and turning clockwise.

● Turn the spanner anticlockwise for Italian-threaded brackets, which you can identify by the 36 x 1 stamped on the fixed cup.

● Ask a good bike shop for help if the fixed cup is hard to remove.

2 **Insert a peg spanner** into two of the holes on the free cup.

● Turn anticlockwise and remove the free cup.

● Take out the axle and look inside the bottom-bracket shell for a plastic sleeve. Remove this sleeve and check that it is intact. Clean it with degreaser and then replace it in the shell.

● Check that the axle is straight by rolling it along a flat surface. If it moves up and down it is bent and must be replaced.

4 **Clean and examine** the two cups now that you have removed them.

● Use a rag soaked in degreaser to clean the cups, bearings, and axle.

● Look at the inside of the cups and the raised bearing surface on the axle. Replace them if they are marked. Replace the bearings, too, if they are marked or no longer round.

5 **Grease the inside of the cups,** press the bearings into the grease, and smear some grease on top of them.

● Fit the fixed cup and bearings into the drive side.

● Insert the axle and screw in the free cup and bearing over the end of the axle, so that the axle spins freely with a very small amount of play.

● Lock the free cup in place with the lockring.

BMX bottom bracket

Many types of bottom bracket are fitted to BMX bikes. The type used in this sequence of steps is similar to the type fitted to many children's bikes.

The biggest difference between this kind of BMX bracket and normal bottom brackets is that the threads securing it in the frame are on the axle and not inside the bottom-bracket shell. The axle has a cup and cone bearing system, a little like an open-bearing hub (see pp.100–1). The drive-side cone, chainring, and axle are made in one piece, and the cranks bolt on to them. This kind of chainset and bottom bracket is called a 3-piece chainset. Screwing the locknut on to the cone needs practising to ensure that the bottom bracket is adjusted successfully.

STEP LOCATOR

Parts of a BMX bottom bracket

Chainring
Drive-side cone
Non-drive side cup
Non-drive side bearings
Non-drive side cone
Axle
Drive-side bearings
Axle threads
Spacing washer
Drive-side cup
Locknut

Toolbox

- Allen key multi-tool
- Peg spanner
- Spanners
- Grease
- Degreaser

Setting up a BMX bottom bracket

1 **Take out the captive bolt** at the centre of the non-drive side crank, then loosen the crank bolt on the side.

4 **Put the newly greased** drive-side bearings back into their cup, then insert the axle so that it sticks out of the non-drive side.

- Put the greased, non-drive side bearings over the axle and into their cup.

- Make sure that the non-drive bearings are sitting square inside their cup.

2 **Remove the crank.** Hold the non-drive cone still with a peg spanner while removing the locknut with a spanner.

● Remove the spacer and the cone and pull out the non-drive bearings from the cup, which is located inside the bottom-bracket shell.

● Inspect, clean, and degrease the cone.

3 **Take out the drive side** of the bottom bracket once you have removed the locknut and cone from the non-drive side.

● Hold the drive side by the drive-side crank and clean and degrease the bearings. Replace any worn bearings and grease the clean bearings.

● Inspect the cups while the drive side is out of the bike. Replace any worn cups or cones.

5 **Put the non-drive cone** and spacer over the axle and screw the cone on to the bearings with the peg spanner. Screw the locknut on to the axle.

● Hold the cone in place against the bearings and screw the locknut down on to it. Then screw the cone back a little to the locknut. A bit of play in the axle is permissible, but too much will throw off the chain.

6 **Put the spacer back** on the non-drive side of the axle and then push the crank back on to it.

● Tighten the captive bolt in the middle of the crank, then tighten the retaining bolt on its side.

PEDALS

There are two types of pedal, flat and clipless. Pedals with open bearings require regular inspection and lubrication. Clipless pedals must be lubricated to ensure easy foot release. Cleats should be correctly fitted to the rider's shoes and regularly inspected for wear.

How they work

The two pedals transfer the push from the rider's legs and feet into both cranks which, in turn, rotate the axle in the bottom bracket. The body of a pedal rotates around an axle and is supported on bearings that are either open or held within a cartridge. The pedal's axle screws into the crank.

Pedals should grip a rider's feet in some way. For example, studs that prevent foot slippage will help a rider who makes frequent stops, such as a commuter in heavy traffic. Some flat pedals are fitted with toe-clips and straps that hold the front of the foot, although they can interfere with the foot as the rider tries to remove it. Clipless pedals hold the foot securely, while releasing it easily whenever the rider wants.

Converting energy
Pedals are the invention that defines cycling. They are the first step in the process of converting human energy into mechanical motion.

FLAT PEDAL ANATOMY

Two bearings on the pedal's axle are held in place by a cone and lockring that screw on to the outer end of the axle. A knurled retainer attaches the pedal body to the axle. The cone (not visible) and the lockring can be adjusted to permit the free rotation of the body around the axle, without any play.

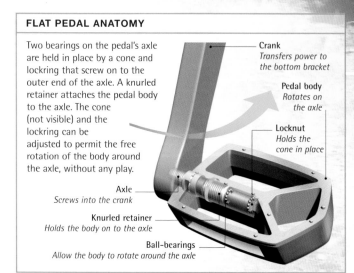

Crank
Transfers power to the bottom bracket

Pedal body
Rotates on the axle

Locknut
Holds the cone in place

Axle
Screws into the crank

Knurled retainer
Holds the body on to the axle

Ball-bearings
Allow the body to rotate around the axle

Pedal
*Connects the rider's foot
to the transmission*

Pedal axle

The axle of a pedal is usually made from steel and the cranks from aluminium alloy. This creates a materials' interface where a chemical reaction can take place between the two metals, so it is important that you coat the threads with grease before you put pedals on your bike. The tools to remove the axles are specific to the make of the pedals, and will be either supplied with the pedals or available at a good bike shop.

Most pedals contain two bearings on which the pedal body revolves around its axle. These sometimes need replacing; in the case of ball-bearings, they need regular cleaning, checking, and greasing.

Pedal axles can be damaged by an impact or during a fall, and a bent axle can cause riding discomfort or even injury. After removing the pedals, rotate their axles by hand, feeling for the tight spots that are evidence of a bent axle.

STEP LOCATOR

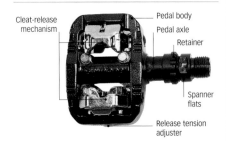

Parts of a pedal

Cleat-release mechanism
Pedal body
Pedal axle
Retainer
Spanner flats
Release tension adjuster

Toolbox

- 15mm bike spanner ● Allen key multi-tool
- Remover tool ● Degreaser ● Grease

Removing and lubricating a pedal axle

1 **Place a spanner** on the flats of the axle to remove a pedal.

● Turn the spanner anticlockwise for the right pedal, which has a right-hand thread, and clockwise for the left pedal, which has a left-hand thread.

● Steady the opposite crank with your hand to give you something to push against.

4 **Lift the axle from the pedal** once you have fully unscrewed the retainer nut.

● Clean the axle with degreaser and inspect it. If the axle is bent, it will need replacing.

● Replace the bearings on the end of the axle if they are worn.

 **Hold the removed pedal,** with the axle upwards, in a vice.

● Remove the axle by using a remover tool that fits over the knurled retainer connecting the axle to the pedal.

Ensure that the remover tool fits snugly on to the retainer. The retainer may be damaged if you do not.

● Place a spanner on the flats of the remover tool in place and turn it to remove the retainer.

● Turn the spanner clockwise for the right axle retainer, which has a left-hand thread, and anticlockwise for the left axle retainer, which has a right-hand thread.

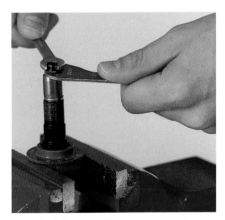

Hold the cone with one spanner and remove the locknut with another. The cone and locknut hold the bearings on the end of the axle.

● Remove the cone, then the old bearings. Clean the end of the axle.

● Set the new bearings in grease and screw the cone back on top of them. Then lock the cone with the locknut.

Grease the inner bearing to prolong its life. If it is worn, the whole axle assembly must be replaced.

● Push some grease down into the bearing after cleaning the axle. To reassemble the pedal, repeat Steps 1–4 in reverse order.

Clipless pedals

Clipless pedals were developed in response to the racing cyclist's need to apply power throughout the entire pedal revolution. They hold the foot to the pedal by locking on to a cleat attached to the sole of the shoe. The mechanism that holds the cleat is spring-loaded – the foot is released by turning the heel outwards.

The release spring is an essential working part and must be kept clean and well lubricated. Use light oils on road pedals

and heavier oils on off-road pedals. Wipe oil from the pedal body to stop your foot from slipping. The mechanism lets the foot pivot around its long axis during each revolution. The oil applied to the release spring is enough to keep the mechanism working well.

Toolbox
- 15mm bike spanner ● Allen key multi-tool
- Degreaser ● Stiff brush ● Oil

OFF-ROAD PEDALS

Off-road pedals are fitted with retention mechanisms on both sides so that the rider's feet can attach to the pedal no matter which way up it is. The pedals also let mud pass through to prevent them from becoming clogged.

Time off-road pedal
The few moving parts of this simple pedal are protected in the body of the pedal. Keep the parts clean and dribble a little heavy oil into the point where the release bar enters the pedal body. If necessary, replace the bearings and axles (see pp.80–1).

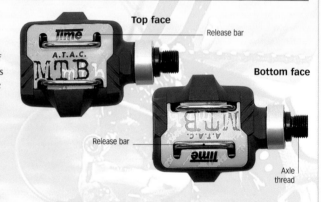

Top face — Release bar
Bottom face
Release bar
Axle thread

Shimano off-road pedal
The open design of this pedal allows good mud clearance but exposes the pedal's retention mechanism to the elements. Clean and degrease the pedals regularly and lubricate the moving parts with a heavy lubricant. The release tension adjuster is on the back plate of this double-sided pedal.

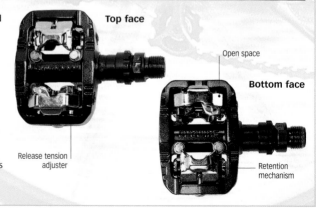

Top face
Open space
Bottom face
Release tension adjuster
Retention mechanism

ROAD PEDALS

Road pedals are light, supportive, and, because of the greater speeds involved in road riding, aerodynamic. They need to engage and release the feet with equal ease as well as holding the foot securely. Ideally, you should be able to adjust them according to how much movement your feet make during pedalling.

Time road pedal
These pedals offer a range of movement that can be adjusted to suit the requirements of individual riders. Keep them well maintained by scrubbing regularly with degreaser, using a stiff brush. Wash this off, then lubricate the release spring with heavier oil, dribbling it from a can.

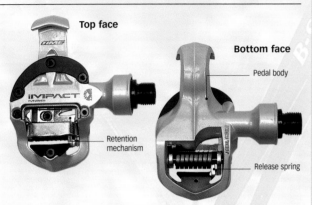

Top face

Bottom face

Pedal body

Retention mechanism

Release spring

Look road pedal
A small Allen bolt in the centre of these easy-to-maintain pedals alters the degree to which the foot can pivot when pedalling. Adjust the foot-release tension via the yellow button on the pedal's back plate. Every now and then, dribble oil between the back plate and body.

Pedal body

Top face

Pivot adjuster

Back plate

Release tension adjuster

Bottom face

Shimano road pedal
The release spring of this pedal is exposed. Degrease and wash the pedals regularly, then lubricate the release spring. The pedal is one-sided, with its release tension adjuster under the release spring. An adjustable pad gives the feet more support. The adjustment bolt is beneath the pedal at the end of its axle.

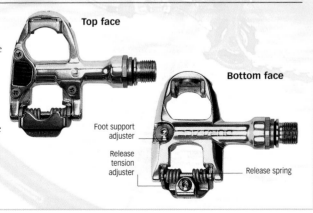

Top face

Bottom face

Foot support adjuster

Release tension adjuster

Release spring

Pedal cleats

Clipless pedals are designed to hold your feet firmly in place, so it is important that the cleats on the pedals are positioned correctly on the sole of your shoes. The right position also enables you to transfer the maximum amount of leg power into the pedals.

Once you have set up the cleats, you might find that your feet try to return to their natural position as you ride. Alter the cleat's angle to accommodate this. However, do not alter its fore and aft position because the position shown here is the most efficient for applying power to the pedals.

The steps in this sequence show an off-road pedal (see pp.82–3), but the principles are the same for road pedals.

STEP LOCATOR

1 2 3 4 5 6

Parts of a pedal cleat

In-shoe threads for fixing bolts

Cleat

Fixing bolts

Recessed cleat plate

Toolbox

- White marker pen • Silicone sealant
- Allen keys • Screwdriver

Fitting a pedal cleat

1 **Put on your cycling shoes** and mark them on the outer side where your foot is widest. This point is usually slightly behind the smallest toe and is in line with the ball of the foot. The aim of setting up a cleat is to make sure that this part of your foot is exactly above the pedal axle when you ride.

4 **Put on your cycling shoes** and sit on your bike, engaging the cleats in the pedals.

- Ask someone to check from the side that the initial mark you made is over the pedal axle.

- Go for a ride and check whether your feet try to turn in or out on the pedals.

Take off your shoes and continue the mark you made with a straight line across the sole of your shoe, from outside to inside. This line must be at right angles to the initial mark and should end on the inner side of the shoe, in line with the initial mark.

Place the cleat on the shoe so that the line runs exactly through its centre. Some cleats are marked to help with this alignment.

● Make sure that the horizontal axis of the cleat is exactly parallel with the line you made.

● Secure the cleat in place with the screws or Allen bolts provided.

Adjust the cleats to accommodate any foot position changes your test ride reveals, but keep the cleat centre over the axle.

● Mark the sole of your shoes all around the cleat, so that you can line it up again.

● Remove the cleat, put anti-seize compound on the screw threads and line the cleat up with the marks you made. Tighten the cleat.

Seal the Allen heads on the bolts that secure the cleats to off-road shoes. These heads can fill with grit, causing them to lose shape and making it difficult to replace the cleats when they wear down. Prevent this by filling the Allen heads with blobs of a silicone sealant available from DIY shops.

4

STEERING AND

Steering gives you control of a bike's handling and direction. Regularly check and maintain the headset, handlebar, wheels, and hubs to safeguard their reliability at all times.

WHEELS

HEADSETS

A headset allows the bike to be steered. The headset must be properly adjusted to allow smooth, safe steering and to prolong its life. The bearings and bearing surfaces need regular inspection and lubrication and anything that is worn must be replaced at once.

How they work

The main function of the headset is to enable the rider to change the direction of the front wheel under any conditions. There are two types of headset, threaded and threadless, and both hold the front fork securely in the head tube, while simultaneously allowing the fork to turn freely.

The headset rotates on bearings, which are held in place by cups, one above the head tube, the other below. For the forks to turn freely, these two cups press on the bearings just enough to prevent any play in the part of the fork known as the steerer tube. The way this pressure (also known as load) is achieved varies between the threaded and threadless headsets.

THREADLESS HEADSET ANATOMY

The stem cap bolt at the top of a threadless headset screws into a star washer below. Some types of threadless headset contain a wedge instead of a star washer. When the bolt is turned with an Allen key, it pushes the stem and spacer down on to the bearings in the top and bottom cups, and pulls up the steerer tube. The bottom cup covers the bearings that sit on the fork crown race at the top of the fork crown. As a result, sufficient load is placed on both bearings to enable the front fork to turn freely but without play.

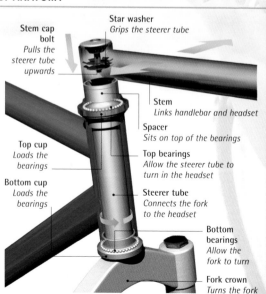

Stem cap bolt
Pulls the steerer tube upwards

Star washer
Grips the steerer tube

Stem
Links handlebar and headset

Spacer
Sits on top of the bearings

Top cup
Loads the bearings

Top bearings
Allow the steerer tube to turn in the headset

Bottom cup
Loads the bearings

Steerer tube
Connects the fork to the headset

Bottom bearings
Allow the fork to turn

Fork crown
Turns the fork

THREADED HEADSET ANATOMY

Screwing the top cup down the thread of the steerer places a load on the top bearings to the point where the forks turn freely but without play. The cup, and consequently the front fork, is then locked in place by a lockring that also screws down the threaded steerer. The stem is attached to the headset by tightening the stem's expander bolt, which pulls up a wedge and jams the stem's quill inside the threaded steerer.

Stem
Links the handlebar and headset

Quill
Fits inside the threaded steerer

Expander bolt
Draws up the wedge

Lockring
Locks the top cup in place

Top bearings
Allow the steerer to turn in the headset

Top cup
Loads the bearings

Wedge
Jams the quill in the steerer

Threaded steerer
Connects the headset to the fork

Bottom bearings
Allow the fork to turn

Handlebar
Steers the front wheel

Headset
Holds the fork in the head tube

Fork
Holds and turns the front wheel

Steering effectively

A headset allows the rider to steer the front wheel effectively and confidently. The handlebar, which is connected to the steerer tube by the stem, turns the fork and the front wheel.

Threadless headset

To determine whether your bike is equipped with a threadless or a threaded headset, look at the stem. If you can see bolts on the side of the part that sits on top of the head tube, it is a threadless headset.

A number of different types of threadless headset can be fitted to modern bikes. These range from the type that has both top and bottom cups, like the traditional headset, to others, such as the headset illustrated here, where the bearing surfaces fit inside the head tube. All the various types of headset work on the same principle and are taken apart in a similar way.

Occasionally, you need to strip down the headset in order to check it for wear and to clean and lubricate the bearings. If you find any cups or bearing surfaces are worn, you will need to replace the whole headset. This job requires specialist equipment and is best left to the experts in a good bike shop.

Adjusting and cleaning a threadless headset

1 **Remove the stem cap bolt** from the centre of the stem cap with an Allen key. This bolt loads the headset to prevent play in it, rather than securing the stem.

STEP LOCATOR

Parts of a threadless headset

Stem cap —
Top bearing cover —
— Stem cap bolt
— Top race
— Bottom cup

Toolbox
- Allen key multi-tool ● Degreaser ● Grease

4 **Lower the fork** and lift off the top spacers and either the top cup or bearing cover, depending on the type of threadless headset.

● Clean, degrease, and look at the bottom bearing. If there are no signs of wear, grease the bearing.

● Take the centring wedge out of the head tube. Clean the bearings, bearing surfaces (*inset*), and bearing cover or top cup . Examine for wear, put new grease on the bearings and re-install.

2 **Loosen the clamp bolts** on the side of the stem once you have removed the cap bolt. The stem and handlebar assembly are now free. It is the stem clamp bolts that secure the stem to the steerer.

3 **Take hold of the front fork,** then lift the stem and handlebar from the steerer. You can leave these to hang out of the way, supported by the brake and gear cables.

5 **Put the fork back** into the head tube and replace the centring wedge, bearing cover, and spacers.

● Put the handlebar and stem back on top of the steerer.

● Load the headset by tightening the stem cap bolt to a point where the handlebar turns freely, but there is no play in the headset. Secure the stem in place by tightening the clamp bolts.

● Apply the front brake and try to push the bike forwards to check that the headset is not loose.

Threaded headset

Older bikes and children's bikes are equipped with threaded headsets. This type of headset is designed to make it easy to raise and lower the stem whenever you want to change the height of the handlebar and adjust your riding position.

The headset's top cup and the locknut that holds it in place are both screwed on to the steerer. The stem is equipped with a shaft, or quill, that fits inside the steerer. For safety reasons, you should never raise a stem above the limit marked on its quill.

On some even older headsets the top cup screws down. Its serrated top edge is held in place by a clamp bolt on a similarly serrated lockring assembly. When the clamp bolt is loosened, the top cup screws off.

Remember to disconnect the brakes before you start working on the headset and make sure that you reconnect them when you have finished. Before the stem is replaced into the steerer of the headset, coat the quill with grease (see pp.30–1).

STEP LOCATOR

1 2 3 4 5 6

Parts of a threaded headset

Spacer
Locknut
Top race
Top cup
SHIMANO ULTEGRA
Bottom cup
SHIMANO ULTEGRA
Fork crown race

Toolbox
- 6mm Allen key ● Grease ● Degreaser ● 30mm and 32mm headset spanners ● Plastic mallet

Servicing a threaded headset

1 **Undo the Allen bolt** in the stem centre and knock it downwards with a plastic mallet to free the steerer. The stem is secured into the steerer by an expander bolt which, as it is tightened, draws a wedge up inside the quill.

● Lift the stem from the steerer.

4 **Degrease all the bearing surfaces** of the top and bottom cups, and of the races. You can access the top bearings by pushing the fork up the head tube and holding it there.

● Inspect the bearing surfaces and if any are damaged, you need to fit a new headset – this is best left to a good bike shop.

2 **Unscrew the locknut** while holding the top cup still with a headset spanner.

● Spread newspaper on the floor to catch loose bearings that may drop out of the top cup.

● Lift off the spacers, then unscrew the top cup upwards from the steerer.

3 **Lower the fork** to reveal the bearings in the bottom cup. Screwing the top cup upwards allows this to happen. Although most headsets have ball-bearings held in cages, watch out for loose bearings that may drop out of the bottom cup. Some headsets have roller bearings – treat these as ball-bearings in the following steps.

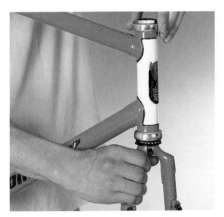

5 **Grease both the top and bottom bearings** or set loose bearings in grease inside each cup.

● Completely unscrew the top cup to remove the bearings. Set the bearings individually in the greased cups and screw the top cup back on. Bearings held in cages can be greased in situ so long as they are not worn out.

6 **Screw the top cup down** on to the top bearings. Replace the spacers and locknut.

● Adjust the top cup so that steering is free.

● Pull the fork to check there is no forward movement in the headset.

● Replace the spacer, hold the top cup with a spanner, and tighten the locknut on to it.

● Replace the stem and handlebar.

HANDLEBARS

Most modern bikes are fitted with either straight or drop handlebars. A rider must be able to rely totally on the handlebar, so for safety reasons, a handlebar must be replaced at once if scratches, stress marks, or cracks develop on the surface.

Straight handlebar

Owners of road bikes sometimes want to change the handlebar to a different shape, often to suit the proportions of their body or because of their cycling needs. Some cyclists want to replace a drop handlebar with a straight, or flat, bar. Others may want to replace their existing straight bars with riser bars, or vice versa. Riser bars, which are fitted to mountain bikes, are straight in the centre, then rise up to become straight where the grips are. They are fitted the same way as a straight handlebar.

The steps in this sequence apply to all straight handlebars, whatever the reason for replacing them. However, when replacing a drop handlebar with a straight bar, it will necessary to swap the brake levers for levers that work with flat or riser bars. Some of these steps will also be useful when fitting new grips, brake levers, gear-shifters, or bar-ends to an existing handlebar.

Parts of a straight handlebar

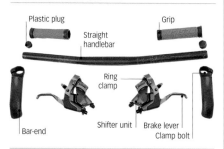

Plastic plug · Grip · Straight handlebar · Ring clamp · Bar-end · Shifter unit · Brake lever · Clamp bolt

Toolbox

- Half-round file ● Emery paper ● Ruler
- Allen key multi-tool ● Hairspray

STEP LOCATOR
1 2 3 4 5

Fitting a straight handlebar

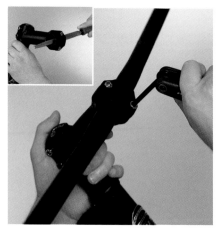

1 **Remove any raised bit of metal** inside the stem clamp with a medium, half-round file (*inset*). Smooth the area with emery paper.

● Place the straight handlebar into the stem clamp and screw in the clamp bolts. Check that the bar is centred before tightening it fully. If you are fitting a riser bar, decide what angle of sweep you want it to be before tightening the bolts.

2 **Secure the ring clamp** of the brake lever to the handlebar. Like road brake levers, off-road levers have a ring clamp that fits over and secures them to the handlebar. Some off-road brake levers have integrated shift levers with only one clamp. However, some are separate so there are two clamps to go over the handlebar.

3 **Spray hairspray** into the handlebar grips to help the grips to slide on to the handlebar. When the hairspray dries, the grips will fit tightly to the handlebars.

4 **Slide the grips** on to the handlebar while they are still wet with hairspray.

● Push the grips further on if you are fitting bar-ends to allow for the width of the bar-end clamp.

● Fit grip-locks to hold the grips in place and prevent them from twisting while you are riding.

5 **Clamp on the bar-ends.** Line them up parallel with the angle of your stem to begin with, then adjust their angle to suit your own preference after riding.

● Put a plastic plug in each end of the handlebar to prevent injury in the event of a fall.

Drop handlebar

Road-riding cyclists often choose to fit a drop handlebar to their bikes so that their bodies can adopt a lower and more aerodynamic position than the more erect posture of a cyclist who uses a straight bar. However, the handlebar should never be positioned so low that the cyclist's breathing is restricted when leaning forwards and holding the bottom of the bar.

A drop handlebar must be replaced immediately if any cracks develop on its surface. The steps in this sequence will show how to replace a drop handlebar and how to fit, and therefore how to re-position, brake levers. Cyclists with larger hands and long arms may prefer to mount the levers lower down the handlebar than the ideal position shown here.

Regularly replace the handlebar tape as shown in Steps 5 and 6, and insert a plug in each end of the handlebar after taping to prevent possible injury in a fall.

STEP LOCATOR

Parts of a drop handlebar

Drop handlebar | Cable groove

Brake lever hood | Rubber cover | Handlebar tape | Brake lever

Toolbox

- Half-round file ● Emery paper
- Allen key multi-tool

Fitting a drop handlebar

1 **Use a medium, half-round file** to remove any raised areas of metal inside the part of the stem that clamps the bar in place. These raised areas can bite into the handlebar, eventually causing them to fracture.

● Smooth the filed surface with emery paper.

4 **Secure the levers** of a Campagnolo brake/shift to the handlebar by tightening a bolt on the outside of the hood with an Allen key. Pull the lever hood cover forwards to access the bolt. The bolt on Shimano levers is further down the outer side of the lever hood so that you need to put your Allen key into a recess under the rubber cover.

2 **Fit the new handlebar** and tighten up the clamp bolts. Before you secure the bolts, try to line up the flat part of the bottom of the handlebar with a point just below the back brake.

3 **Slide the steel ring** of the brake lever over the handlebar. This ring clamps the lever to the handlebar.

- Attach the bolt in the brake lever hood to the screw thread on the ring and tighten.

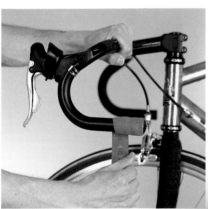

6 **Pull the cover** of the brake lever hood forwards and place a short length of tape over each steel ring.

- Wind the tape in one turn from the bottom to the top of the lever hood. When you reach the top of the handlebar, secure the tape with insulating tape.

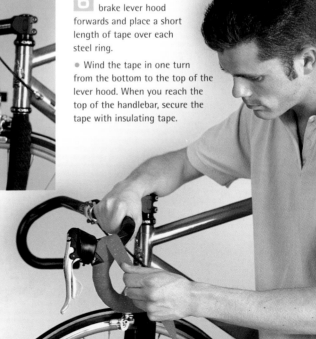

5 **Start taping** at one end of the handlebar.

- Wind upwards, covering half of the previous turn with each subsequent turn.

- Keep the tape tight at all times.

HUBS

There are two types of hub, open-bearing and cartridge. The cones and bearings of open-bearing hubs must be adjusted to let the hub spin freely, with little play. The bearings in both types of hub need regular checking and lubricating.

How they work

The hub allows the wheel to revolve. Quick-release mechanisms or nuts secure the axle into the bike's frame. The axle remains static while the hub body spins around on bearings. Spokes run from the hub's flanges to the rim of the wheel – as the hub spins, so does the rim.

The transmission transfers the rider's power from the pedals to the rear wheel, while the front wheel is essentially pushed along by the revolutions of the rear. The gears on a bike are located on the rear hub, either as a hub-gear unit or as multiple sprockets in the case of derailleur gears.

The freewheel mechanism, which is also on the rear hub, allows a rider to cease pedalling while the bike is in motion – for example, on a downhill stretch of road. This mechanism is part of the hub in both hub gears and hubs with cassette sprockets.

Minimizing friction
Free-spinning hubs are an essential part of an efficient bike. Their bearings must create as little friction as possible, so as not to slow the rider's forward progress.

EXPLODED CARTRIDGE HUB

The axle of a cartridge hub is not threaded, so the bearings are pushed on to each end of the axle and covered by a seal. When the hub is assembled, the bearings sit in the hub body, just to the outside of the flanges, with the axle running through them. Lockrings ensure that everything is held in place.

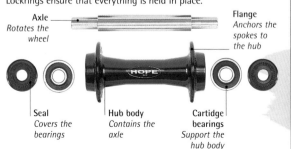

Axle
Rotates the wheel

Flange
Anchors the spokes to the hub

Seal
Covers the bearings

Hub body
Contains the axle

Cartridge bearings
Support the hub body

OPEN-BEARING FRONT HUB ANATOMY

The body on an open-bearing front hub spins on ball-bearings
that are set within, and at each end of, the hub body. Each set
of bearings is held in place by a cone (not visible) that is screwed
down on the thread at the end of the axle. A locknut (not visible)
locks the cone in place on the same thread. If the hub is held by a
quick-release mechanism, the axle is hollow to allow the quick-
release skewer to go through it.

Axle
*Remains static
as the wheel
revolves*

Hub body
*Rotates
around
the axle*

**Ball-
bearings**
*Support the
hub body*

**Quick-release
skewer**
*Locks the axle
in place*

Open-bearing
front hub
*Allows the wheel to
revolve smoothly*

Open-bearing hub

Hubs are available, like bottom brackets, in two types – open-bearing or cartridge. The open-bearing hubs require much more maintenance than the cartridge type (*see pp.102–3*), since their bearings need regular inspection, cleaning, and regreasing. As a result, the ability to strip down and service an open-bearing hub is a skill that can be used repeatedly.

The following steps will help you to remove an axle and a freehub, as well as regrease and retighten the bearings. They can be applied to a Shimano front or rear hub and a Campagnolo front hub. However, leave servicing a Campagnolo rear hub to the experts at a bike shop because it requires specialist tools.

Before tackling the steps in this sequence, the cassette or block should be removed (*see pp.66–7* and *pp.68–9*).

STEP LOCATOR

Parts of an open-bearing hub

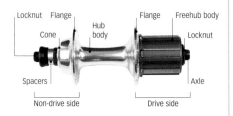

Locknut   Flange   Flange   Freehub body

Cone   Hub body   Locknut

Spacers   Axle

Non-drive side   Drive side

Toolbox

- 15mm and 16mm cone spanners (Shimano)
- 13mm and 14mm cone spanners (Campagnolo)
- Grease ● Grease gun (optional)
- Allen key multi-tool ● Adjustable spanner
- 8mm or 10mm Allen key

Overhauling an open-bearing hub

1 **Remove the locknut** on the drive side with a spanner while holding the non-drive side cone with a cone spanner. Some locknuts can be removed with an ordinary spanner, others with an Allen key.

● Keep holding the non-drive side cone with the cone spanner and remove the drive-side cone with another cone spanner.

4 **Take out all the ball-bearings** from each side and clean them with degreaser.

● Replace ball-bearings that are scored or have flat spots on their surface.

● Insert a layer of grease into each groove, or race, where the ball-bearings sit.

● Return the ball-bearings to each race, pressing down firmly so the grease holds them in place.

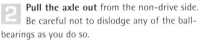 **Pull the axle out** from the non-drive side. Be careful not to dislodge any of the ball-bearings as you do so.

● Clean the cones and axle and then inspect them for damage. Check to see if the axle is bent by rolling it on a flat surface and looking for any irregular motion. Replace damaged cones or bent axles immediately.

Insert an Allen key into the 8mm or 10mm Allen bolt located in the centre of the freehub. This bolt holds the freehub body on to the axle.

● Turn the key anticlockwise to remove the freehub. You may need a bit of force to loosen this bolt so use an Allen key with a long handle for extra leverage.

Fit the new hub body or the cleaned old one by reversing Step 3.

● Re-insert the axle from the non-drive side.

● Tighten the drive cone up to the bearings and check that the axle spins freely with minimal play.

● Lock the cone into position with the locknut.

● Use the cone spanners to check that the non-drive cone is tight against its locknut.

Cartridge hub

Cartridge hubs offer many of the advantages of cartridge-bearing bottom brackets – for example, they keep out water and dirt, increasing the life of the bearing. However, unlike many cartridge bottom brackets, you can change bearings when they wear out. Replacing the bearings is a straightforward task that requires special drifts to drive out the old bearings and drive in the new.

Check the bearings by removing the wheel from the bike and spinning it while holding the axle. If you feel any roughness the bearings are worn. Excessive play of the hub on the axle is also a sign of wear.

Only the hub is shown in these steps, but you will deal with the whole wheel. You can also follow these steps to replace a bent or broken axle – although rare, it can happen if a bike hits a bump in the road and the rider is not prepared for it, or when landing jumps on a mountain bike or a BMX.

STEP LOCATOR

Parts of a cartridge hub (front)

Hub flanges

Axle   Hub body   Bearing

Lockring

Toolbox

● Plastic mallet ● Vice ● Drifts (suitable for make of hub – check manufacturer's instructions)
● Allen key multi-tool (optional)

Overhauling a cartridge hub

1 **Remove the seals** from each side of the hub axle. Some seals are retained by a lockring that is secured with a grub screw; others just require prising off.

● Remember how they look in situ and where they fit as you will need to put them back in exactly the same position.

4 **Insert the first new cartridge bearing** by offering the bearing square to the hub and driving it home with a wider drift.

● Knock the bearings in gently. Although it can sometimes take a bit of force to knock the old bearings out, it should not take too much force to position the new ones in place.

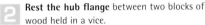

Rest the hub flange between two blocks of wood held in a vice.

• Tap the axle down with a plastic mallet. Be confident when using the mallet, as you may have to be forceful.

• Drive the axle through the upper bearing with a drift. This is a metal cylinder with the same diameter as the centre of the cartridge bearing.

Take out the axle from the hub body with a bearing still attached to it.

• Lay this bearing on the wooden blocks and drive the axle through.

• Drift the other bearing out of the hub body, as in Step 2. Do this from behind the bearing, by tapping the drift from the same side of the hub from which you removed the axle.

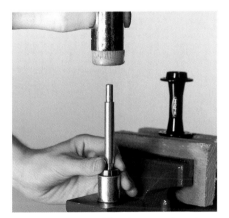

Push the second bearing on to the axle, then place the drift on to a flat surface, such as the flat portion of the vice. If you are not using a vice, place a piece of thick metal on the work surface or even the floor. The surface must be strong enough to absorb the mallet blows.

• Lay the bearing on the drift and tap the axle fully into the bearing.

Lower the hub down on to the axle. Make sure that the axle is through the middle of the bearing you have already fixed inside the hub.

• Use the drifts to tap the hub down so that the axle goes all the way into the bearing.

• Replace the seals and spacers. Secure the lockrings on to the axle. The grooves on the seals must snap back into place or the seals will not work.

WHEELS

Quick-release mechanisms help to remove and replace a wheel quicker than ever before. The tyres are the component that make contact with the ground. Match the tyres on your bike to the prevailing riding conditions and always be ready to replace worn-out tyres.

Quick-release wheels

Removing and refitting a wheel is a straightforward task, but if any of the following steps are overlooked, the wheel may come loose and compromise the rider's safety. The steps are for wheels with quick-release levers that secure them in the drop-outs (the recess in the frame into which the axle fits). For bikes with axle nuts, loosening and tightening with a spanner corresponds to unlocking and locking the quick-release lever.

Levers are labelled "locked" or "closed" on the side facing the cyclist when the wheel is secure, and "unlocked" or "open" when it is not. Check levers are locked before each ride, and during a ride if disc brakes are fitted.

The rim brake needs to be released on the wheel being removed. For V-brakes, unhook the cable from its cradle; for cantilevers unhook the straddle wire from the left brake arm; for callipers, use the quick-release lever.

Parts of the quick-release system

Fork

Quick-release lever

Quick-release body

Wheel drop-out

Toolbox

• Spanners for wheels with axle nuts

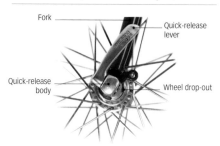

STEP LOCATOR

Removing a rear wheel

1 **Release the brake,** shift the chain on to the smallest sprocket and pull the quick-release lever away from the bike into the unlocked position. Some quick-release levers are shaped so that they bend towards the frame when in the locked position. This provides a visual check if nothing is printed on the lever.

Removing a front wheel

1 **Release the brake.** Pull the quick-release lever to the unlocked position. If the drop-out has safety lips, the wheel will not come out of the fork at this stage. These safety lips prevent the wheel falling out in the unlikely event of the lever becoming unlocked while you ride.

● Use your fingers to unscrew the nut on the opposite side of the lever until the quick-release clears the safety lip.

2 **Lift up the bike** to allow the wheel to drop out of the fork.

● Replace the front wheel by reversing Step 1.

● Push the quick-release lever behind the left fork leg to prevent anything catching it and opening it accidentally.

● Reconnect the brake once the wheel is locked.

2 **Hook the chain** out of the way and on to the peg situated on the inner side of the right seat stay (if there is one).

● Pull the rear mech back and then lift up the rear of the bike.

● Give the tyre a sharp blow from above with the heel of your hand if the wheel does not drop forwards and out of the frame.

3 **Replace the wheel** by introducing the hub axle to the drop-outs.

● Hook the chain on to the smallest sprocket, then push or pull the wheel backwards.

● Line up the tyre exactly in the middle of the chainstays as you hold the wheel straight.

● Push the quick-release lever into the locked position to secure the wheel. Reconnect the brake.

Puncture repair

When you are out on a ride, it is much easier to replace a punctured inner tube with an intact tube rather than painstakingly mend the puncture. At home, you can repair the punctured tube with adhesive and a patch. It is still a good idea to carry a repair kit on every ride, because you might be unlucky enough to get a second puncture and be forced to repair the tube outdoors.

The main point to remember about mending a puncture is not to rush any of the stages. If you patiently give the glue time to dry, closely examine the inside of the tyre, and carefully refit the tube, then you will be rewarded with a successful repair. If you miss anything or trap the inner tube, you may get another puncture.

STEP LOCATOR

1 2 3 4 5

Parts of a wheel

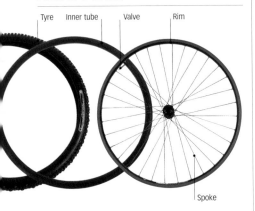

Tyre   Inner tube   Valve   Rim

Spoke

Toolbox

● Tyre levers ● Crayon ● Sandpaper ● Chalk
● Patch adhesive ● Repair patches

Mending a punctured inner tube

1 **Take the wheel out** of the bike. Place one tyre lever under the tyre bead and lift it off the rim. Hook this lever around one of the spokes.

● Insert another lever under the tyre near to the hooked lever. Push the second lever forwards and run it around the whole circumference of the rim to remove one side of the tyre.

● Remove the inner tube from the rim.

4 **Take the tyre off the wheel,** turn it inside out and thoroughly check the inner surface.

● Remove anything that is sticking through the tyre by pulling it out from the outside of the tyre.

2 **Inflate the tube** a little and listen for the sound of escaping air. Locate the hole, mark it with a crayon, and let the air out of the tube.

• Spread a thin layer of adhesive over and around the hole (*inset*). Allow time for it to become tacky.

• Peel the foil from the patch. Press the patch firmly on to the adhesive for over a minute. Make sure that the edges are flat.

3 **Use a small piece of sandpaper** to dust some chalk over the patch to prevent excess adhesive from sticking to the inside of the tyre.

• Leave the tube for a few minutes to make sure that the adhesive has dried.

5 **Put one side of the tyre** fully back on to the rim. Slightly inflate the tube, insert the valve into the hole in the rim, and then work the tube back inside the tyre.

• Put the other side of the tyre in place by pushing the valve upwards, then lifting the section of tyre next to the valve over the rim. Work the tyre back around the rim.

• Check that the tyre has not trapped the tube underneath it before fully inflating the tube. To do this, pinch the tyre together and look around the whole circumference of the wheel.

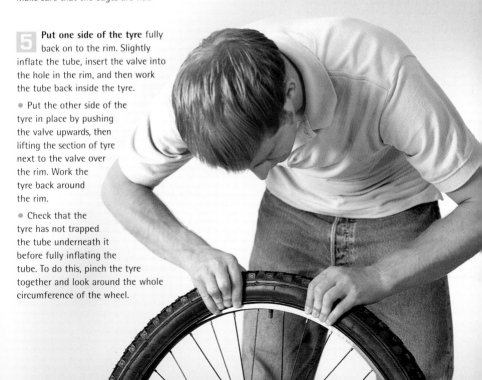

Spokes and rims

The steps in this sequence explain how to replace a single broken spoke and how to true a wheel, a term for straightening the rim of a wheel. However, replacing multiple spokes, replacing spokes in non-standard wheels, and truing a wheel that has been buckled by some kind of impact are jobs that are best left to the experts in a good bike repair shop.

It is essential to true the wheel after replacing a broken spoke because the wheel rim is kept straight by the combined pull of all the spokes acting on it. If one spoke breaks, its pull is missed and the rim as a whole goes out of line.

A wheel jig is needed to true a wheel properly. This tool holds the wheel securely in place and its jaws provide a reference point either side of the rim to help judge how out of line the wheel has become. Bringing it in line is a matter of tightening the new spoke until it reaches the same tension as the old spoke.

STEP LOCATOR

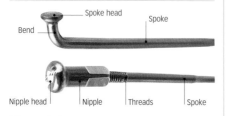

Parts of a spoke

Spoke head
Spoke
Bend

Nipple head | Nipple | Threads | Spoke

Toolbox
- Spoke key • Wheel jig
- Long-nosed pliers

Replacing a spoke and truing a wheel

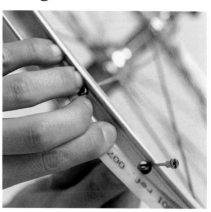

1 **Remove the wheel** and take off the tyre and inner tube.

• Lift up the rim tape next to the broken spoke and push the spoke upwards and out of the rim. If the head of the spoke is broken, measure the broken spoke so you can buy the correct length to replace it. If the break occurred in another place, measure the two pieces to get the right length.

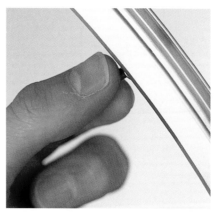

4 **Screw the nipple** on to the spoke. For the first few turns you can use your fingers.

• Go back to Step 2 and check that it is laced exactly the same way as the spoke four along from it. If it is not laced properly, tensioning the spoke in Steps 5 and 6 could damage the wheel.

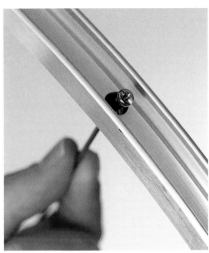

2 **Insert the new spoke,** threads first, into the hub flange from the opposite side to its two neighbours.

● Lace the new spoke into the wheel, under and over the neighbouring spokes. To do this, look at the spoke four along and lace the new spoke exactly the same way.

3 **Push the nipple** of the new spoke through the rim hole from inside the rim and screw it on to the spoke.

● Remove the rim tape to make it easier to fit the nipple on to the new spoke.

● Check the rim tape – if you see any splits, or if it is frayed, replace the tape.

5 **Put the wheel into a wheel jig** and take up the remaining slack on the spoke nipple by tightening it with a spoke key. Make sure that the spoke key is precisely the right size for the nipples on the wheel.

● Stop short of making the spoke as tight as its neighbours at this stage.

6 **Use small, measured turns** of the spoke key to tension the spoke.

● Rotate the wheel so that the nipple of the new spoke is between the jaws of your jig.

● Note how out of line the rim is, then give the nipple a one-quarter tightening turn and check again between the jaws. Repeat and check each quarter turn until the rim is straight.

5

ADJUSTING YOUR

BRAKES

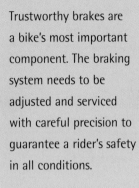

Trustworthy brakes are a bike's most important component. The braking system needs to be adjusted and serviced with careful precision to guarantee a rider's safety in all conditions.

RIM BRAKES

Rim brakes stop a bike by contacting the rim of the wheels. Pads must be checked to ensure that they contact the rim fully and at the same time, and replaced when they are worn. Brake cables must be checked and lubricated regularly.

How they work

The three most common types of rim brake, V-brake, cantilever, and calliper, work in a similar way. A lever pulls a cable, which causes the two brake arms to move towards each other simultaneously. This action brings the two pads into contact with the braking surface of the wheel rim. Springs cause the arms to move back when the lever is released. Cantilever brakes distribute the cable's pull via a straddle wire. The inner cable in a V-brake and calliper pulls one arm, while the outer, in resisting this pull, effectively pushes the other arm.

Braking safely
Rim brakes must be set up properly and maintained to very high standards if they are to work effectively and safely on any surface and in all conditions.

V-BRAKE ANATOMY

The cable of a V-brake is attached to a brake arm by a cable-clamp bolt. When pulled, the cable pulls this arm towards the rim. At the same time, the cable-guide tube, which is an extension of the cable outer, pushes the other arm inwards. The two arms pivot around the brake bosses, pushing the brake pads against the braking surface on the rim. Once the cable's pull is released, springs around the pivot bolts push both brake arms apart.

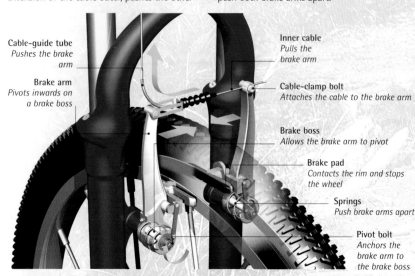

Cable-guide tube
Pushes the brake arm

Brake arm
Pivots inwards on a brake boss

Inner cable
Pulls the brake arm

Cable-clamp bolt
Attaches the cable to the brake arm

Brake boss
Allows the brake arm to pivot

Brake pad
Contacts the rim and stops the wheel

Springs
Push brake arms apart

Pivot bolt
Anchors the brake arm to the brake boss

Brake lever
Pulls the cable

Brake arm
Moves the brake pads towards the rim

Brake pad
Slows down the wheel

BRAKE LEVER ANATOMY

When the rider applies the brake lever it pulls the nipple of the inner cable. As it leaves the lever, the brake cable runs inside a cable outer, which leads to a barrel adjuster. The adjuster allows the brake travel to be fine-tuned.

Nipple
Fixes inner cable to brake lever

Inner cable
Links the brake arm to the brake lever

Barrel adjuster
Adjusts brake travel

Cable outer
Resists the pull on the cable

Brake lever
Pulls the nipple

Drop handlebar brake cable

Brake cables on a drop handlebar need to be changed at regular intervals, although this depends on how much the road bike is used. For a heavily used bike, change the brake cables every two months; for a bike ridden lightly two or three times a week, change the brake cables once a year.

The steps in this sequence are performed on the back brake. Replacing a cable on the front brake follows the same principles, but there are no cable guides to thread through.

Brake levers that fit a drop handlebar require a brake cable with a pear nipple. Always keep a new cable in the toolbox or workshop as a spare. A rear cable can be cut to fit the front as well. Once the cable has been removed, remember to put a few drops of lubricant on the pivots around which the brake lever moves, and spray some oil into the tube inside the lever hood where the cable is inserted.

STEP LOCATOR

Parts of a brake lever and brake cable

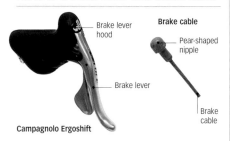

Brake lever hood

Brake cable

Pear-shaped nipple

Brake lever

Brake cable

Campagnolo Ergoshift

Toolbox

- Long-nosed pliers ● Cable cutters
- Allen key multi-tool ● Fine round file

Replacing road bike brake cables

1 **Loosen the cable–clamp bolt** on the brake calliper. Remove the old cable by pulling its nipple from the lever hood with long-nosed pliers.

● Note exactly where the cable fits in the lever hood to allow you to fit the new one easily.

● Remove the part of the cable that is still clamped to the calliper if the cable you are replacing has broken.

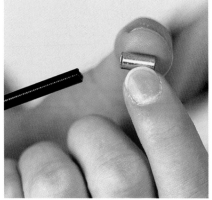

4 **Fit each length** of cable outer with a metal ferrule at both ends. When you apply the brake, ferrules prevent the cable outers from being pulled through the cable guides on the frame.

● Make sure that each ferrule is fully pushed home. Put a little oil on the end of the ferrule to help it slide into place and wipe off any excess.

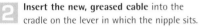 **Insert the new, greased cable** into the cradle on the lever in which the nipple sits.

● Thread the cable into the tube in the lever hood. Push it in and look for it coming out of the back of the lever hood. Now pull it through the lever hood from behind.

● Make sure that the nipple is seated in the brake lever cradle when the cable is all the way through.

Cut the new cable outer to length with good-quality cable cutters. Measure the old outer and cut the new one to the same length.

● Always cut between the spirals of the cable outer.

● Dribble oil into the cable outer, holding it while the oil runs down to coat the inside.

● Renew cable outers at regular intervals.

Thread the cable through the first length of cable outer and the first cable guide.

● Pull the cable all the way through and insert it into the next guide, then the next outer.

● Push the cable outers firmly into the guides, to ensure there is no slack when applying the brakes.

● Use a fine round file to file out any tight cable guides. Do not file more than you have to.

Pull the cable through the cable-clamp bolt on the calliper until each brake pad is about 2mm from the wheel rim.

● Hold the cable and tighten the clamp bolt.

● If the brakes have a quick release, make sure that it is in the closed position before you tighten the clamp bolt. Shimano quick releases are on the calliper and Campagnolo quick releases on the lever.

Straight handlebar brake cable

Replacing the brake cable inners and outers is a job that should be done fairly often on a mountain bike – about once every six to 12 months. They also need replacing if they start fraying and become worn. The hybrid bike in this sequence has V-brakes, but some mountain bikes are equipped with cantilever brakes. Fitting cables is similar for both.

Brake cables also require regular cleaning and lubricating, especially if the bike has been ridden consistently in wet weather. All brake levers that fit on to a straight or riser handlebar require a cable with a barrel nipple.

Regardless of the manufacturer, the barrel nipple fits into the brake lever in the same way. Remember to use ferrules on both ends of every length of new outer cable. Crimp a cable tidy on the end of the cable, once everything is secure and working as it should.

In these steps the tyre is removed from the wheel to show clearly what is happening.

STEP LOCATOR

Parts of a brake lever and a brake cable

Brake lever
Ring clamp
Reach adjuster
Brake lever
Barrel adjuster

Brake cable
Nipple
Brake cable

Toolbox

- Long-nosed pliers ● Cable cutters
- Allen key multi-tool ● Cable pullers (optional)

Replacing V-brake cables on a hybrid bike

1 **Undo the cable-clamp bolt** on the brake. Note where the nipple sits in the cradle that is part of the lever and remove the cable from inside the brake lever by pulling it out with long-nosed pliers.

- Check the outer cables. If they are not worn, you can use them again. Flush them out with degreaser and dribble oil into them.

4 **Attach the cable** to the brake arm by inserting it in the cable guide tube and then pull it through the cable-clamp bolt.

- Keep the cable under tension and check that each length of cable outer is properly seated in the cable guides.

- Pull the cable to bring the brake pads closer to the rim. Tighten the clamp bolt when the pads are about 2mm from the rim.

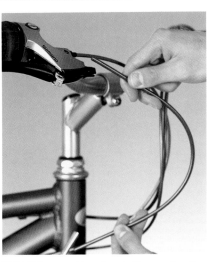

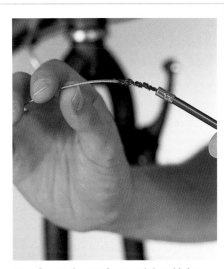

2 **Cut new cable outers** to the same length as the outers you removed or measure them up on your bike and trim as needed. Buy cable outer either in a roll or in pre-cut lengths with inners in a cable kit. The pre-cut lengths may be too long for your bike so you may still have to cut to fit.

● Dribble oil into each cable outer and push a metal ferrule on to each end.

3 **Grease the new inner** and thread it into the brake lever. When it shows through the barrel adjuster, pull it from this side of the lever until the nipple is seated in the lever cradle.

● Thread the cable through the lengths of cable outer and seat the cable outers in the cable guides of the frame.

5 **Pull the brake lever** until the brake is fully applied. This ensures that all cable outers are bedded in and all bolts are tight.

● Undo the cable-clamp bolt and repeat Step 4 if the cable slips through the clamp bolt or a ferrule is not seated properly.

6 **Cut off any excess cable** once the cables are bedded in.

● Leave about 4cm (1½in) of free cable after the cable-clamp bolt.

● Crimp a cable tidy on the end of the cable to prevent it from fraying.

Calliper brake

Maintaining calliper brakes is a question of regularly checking the action of the brake lever. If you have to pull it too far before the brake bites, the brake needs adjusting. Check the brake pads for wear and alignment, and ensure that they contact the braking surface of the rims simultaneously.

How far the lever has to be pulled before the brake comes on depends on the rider. People with smaller hands may prefer more travel in the lever before the brake bites, because they will pull with more strength the closer the lever is to the handlebar.

Apart from their quick releases, all dual-pivot calliper brakes (such as the Shimano brakes shown here) work in the same way, regardless of the manufacturer. This means that you should be able to apply these steps to your bike, whatever its brakes.

STEP LOCATOR

Parts of a calliper brake

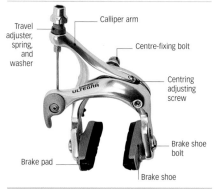

Travel adjuster, spring, and washer

Calliper arm

Centre-fixing bolt

Centring adjusting screw

Brake shoe bolt

Brake pad

Brake shoe

Toolbox

- Full set of Allen keys or Allen key multi-tool
- Long-nosed pliers (optional)

Adjusting a calliper brake

1 **Periodically check for pad wear**. If the pads are wearing down towards half their original depth they must be replaced.

- Undo the Allen key pad retainer and push out the pad. If the pad and shoe are a complete piece, replace the whole unit, releasing the old pad and fitting the new one with a 5mm Allen key.

3 **Pull the brake on** with the brake lever and check to see if both pads simultaneously come into contact with the braking surface on the rim of the wheel.

- Make sure that both sides are working together by turning an adjustment screw on the side of the caliper with an Allen key. This process is called "centring" the brakes.

Using quick-release mechanisms

2 **Adjust the brake pads** so they are directly in line with the braking surface of the rim.

• Release the 5mm Allen bolt on the pad and line the pad up with the braking surface.

• Look for pad wear at this point. Pads that have been set too low will develop a lip and will need to be replaced.

1 **Use a quick-release mechanism** when the adjusted brake pads are so close to the rim that it is impossible to remove the wheel. Campagnolo and Shimano calliper brakes are equipped with different quick-release systems.

• Lift the small lever on the cable-fixing bolt to make Shimano calliper brake pads move away from the rim. After replacing the wheel, lower the lever.

4 **Adjust the brake travel** if you have to pull the brake lever back a long way towards the handlebar before the wheel stops moving.

• Undo the cable-fixing bolt and squeeze the sides of the calliper until the pads nearly touch the rim. The brake cable will then move through the fixing bolt.

• Tighten the bolt and release the calliper.

1 **Press the small button** at the side of the brake lever to move Campagnolo calliper brake pads away from the rim.

• Restore the pads to their original position by pulling the brake lever towards the handlebar until the brakes are on and then push the small button back.

V-brake

V-brakes are fitted to most new mountain bikes because they give good stopping power. Maintaining brake performance is crucial because of the harsh conditions to which mountain bikes are sometimes subjected, so knowing how to adjust the brakes at home and out on the trail is very important.

Pad alignment and brake travel need to be checked and adjusted regularly to keep them working properly. Bear in mind that as soon as you ride off-road you will increase brake pad wear. Even a single ride can render already worn pads useless, so change them before they need it.

Adjustment in the workshop, especially pad alignment, is best performed with the tyre removed, since off-road tyres are bulky and can be in the way. Wheels must run true before setting up brakes (see pp.108–9).

STEP LOCATOR

Parts of a V-brake

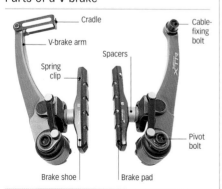

Cradle

Cable-fixing bolt

V-brake arm

Spacers

Spring clip

Pivot bolt

Brake shoe

Brake pad

Toolbox
- Full set of Allen keys or Allen key multi-tool
- Cross-head screwdriver • Cable puller (optional)

Adjusting a V-brake

1 **Check that the stopper pin** on each brake arm is seated in the same hole on the brake bosses. If it is not, remove the pivot bolt, slide the brake arm off the boss, and put the pin into the correct hole.

- Replace the pivot bolt and re-tighten it. If you notice that the brake boss was dry with the arm removed, smear a little grease on it.

4 **Re-tension the brakes** by hooking the cable back in its cradle.

- Check that the gap between each brake pad and the rim of the wheel is 1mm.

- Undo the cable-fixing bolt with an Allen key and pull the cable through until the 1mm gap is achieved. Then tighten the cable-fixing bolt.

2 **Press the brake arms together**. If they are not vertical when the pads touch the rim, rearrange the spacers either side of the pads until they are vertical.

● Release the brakes by unhooking the cable-guide tube from the cradle. Do this when you remove the wheel with correctly adjusted V-brakes.

3 **Undo the brake-pad fixing bolt,** remove the pad and shoe assembly, and swap the spacers around.

● Check the pads. If they are worn, remove the pad-retaining clip, push the old pad from the shoe, and replace it with a new one.

● Line up the pads so that they hit the rim with their entire braking surface, and are parallel to it. Then tighten the fixing bolts.

5 **Use a cross-head screwdriver** to tighten or loosen the centring screw on each brake arm. The aim is to make both arms move an equal distance before the pad touches the rim when you apply the brake lever.

● The tension on each screw should ideally be even, since there is an equal number of spacers on either side of the brake arm.

6 **Screw out the barrel adjuster** on the brake lever to reduce brake travel and make the brakes feel more responsive.

● Screw the adjuster outwards to reduce brake travel and create firmer braking. This technique is quick and easy to perform, and is especially useful for riding in the wet when brake pads can wear down rapidly.

Cantilever brake

Cantilever brakes work with the brake levers that fit dropped handlebars, whereas V-brakes do not. This is why touring and cyclo-cross bikes are fitted with cantilevers. Cantilevers were the predecessors of V-brakes, so they may also be fitted to older mountain and hybrid bikes.

Keep cantilever brakes running smoothly by regularly checking the pads for wear and adjusting the pad alignment and brake travel.

The cable of the cantilever brake shown in these steps is clamped to one brake arm and the straddle wire running off it attaches to the other arm. On some older cantilever brakes, the brake cable is attached to a straddle. This hooks the straddle wire that transfers the cable's pull to both brake arms and needs regular adjustment (see *Step 1 Adjusting a BMX U-brake, pp.124–25*).

STEP LOCATOR

Parts of a cantilever brake

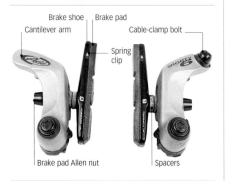

Brake shoe   Brake pad
Cantilever arm   Cable-clamp bolt
                        Spring
                        clip
Brake pad Allen nut   Spacers

Toolbox

- 5mm Allen key ● Grease gun (optional)
- Grease

Adjusting a cantilever brake

1 **Disconnect the straddle wire** by pushing the cantilever arm to which it is attached towards the wheel with one hand. At the same time, unhook the nipple on the straddle with the other hand.

- Undo the pivot bolts that attach the cantilever arms to the frame bosses.
- Remove the cantilever arms.

1 mm

2 mm

4 **Angle the pads** so that the front of each pad hits the rim before the rear when the brakes are applied – this is called "toe in".

- Loosen the pad-fixing bolt and place a cosmetic emery board between the rear of the pad and the rim. Apply the brakes and then tighten the bolt. Release the brakes and remove the emery board. Ideally, the front of the pad should be 1mm from the rim and the rear 2mm.

2 **Clean the exposed frame bosses** with a cloth soaked in degreaser, then lubricate with a light grease, not a heavy-duty industrial grease. Use a grease gun if you have one.

● Bolt both arms back on to the bosses, making sure that the stopper pins are inserted into the same hole on each boss.

● Replace the pivot bolts and then tighten them to hold the brake arms to the bosses.

3 **Check the pads.** If one is worn or badly aligned, undo the pad-fixing bolt with an Allen key and remove the pad/shoe assembly.

● Remove the spring clip from the brake shoe and slide out the worn pad. Slide in a new pad and replace the spring clip.

● Return the assembly to the brake arm, line up the pad so that its entire surface contacts the rim, and is parallel with it, then tighten the bolt.

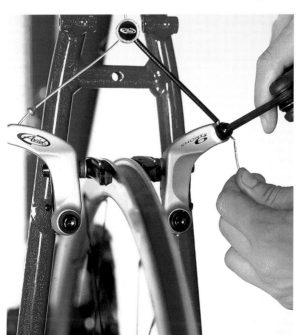

5 **Undo the brake-cable clamp** to achieve the proper spacing from the pad to the rim.

● Pull the cable through the clamp until the front of each brake pad is 1mm from the rim. Tighten the clamp bolt.

● Pull the brake lever to see if both brake arms contact the rim simultaneously. If they do not, screw the centring screws in or out on each arm until they do.

Alternative brake designs

Two alternative brake designs are commonly fitted to some new bikes. These are the side-pull calliper brakes used on children's bikes and the U-brakes fitted on BMX bikes. Side-pulls work in much the same way as callipers (see pp.118–19), while U-brakes resemble cantilevers (see pp.122–23).

Before buying replacement cables for either of these types of brake, first check the kind of nipple that is presently used on the bike in question. Some levers on children's bikes and older bikes require pear nipples, while other levers need barrel nipples. When a new cable is fitted to a side-pull calliper brake, leave the barrel adjuster at the halfway point of its range.

STEP LOCATOR

Parts of a side-pull brake and a U-brake

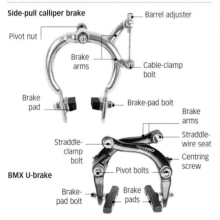

Side-pull calliper brake

Barrel adjuster

Pivot nut

Brake arms

Cable-clamp bolt

Brake pad

Brake-pad bolt

Brake arms

Straddle-wire seat

Straddle-clamp bolt

Centring screw

Pivot bolts

BMX U-brake

Brake-pad bolt

Brake pads

Toolbox

- Allen key multi-tool ● Long-nosed pliers
- Spanners

Adjusting a side-pull calliper brake

1 **Loosen the cable–clamp bolt** and pull the cable through until the brake pads are closer to the rim. This compensates for pad wear.

- Screw in the barrel adjuster to move the pads away or screw it out to move them closer.

- Replace pads that are worn below half their depth by undoing the pad bolt and fitting a new pad or shoe unit in their place.

Adjusting a BMX U-brake

1 **Undo the straddle clamp** bolt and pull the brake cable through the straddle with long-nosed pliers to take up the pad wear. Then tighten the nut.

2 **Use an Allen key** to adjust the centring screw on each brake arm if the pads do not contact the rim at the same time. Screw in to move the pad away from the rim.

2 Centre the brakes if one brake pad is contacting the rim before the other.

● Undo the brake's pivot nut that holds it in place and is located behind the fork crown.

● Hold the calliper so that both pads are an equal distance from the rim and tighten the pivot nut.

3 Undo the pad bolts, line up the pads and tighten the bolt so that the brake pads contact the rim directly in line with it. Do this when you replace worn pads, too.

● Inspect the pads regularly. If you find any ridges on them, replace the pads (see Step 1) and then line them up as described above, so that the whole of their surface contacts the rim.

3 Line up or replace pads in the same way as calliper brakes (see pp.118–19). Replace the brake pads by removing the pad bolts and fitting new pad and shoe units.

● To reconnect the brake, pinch the brake arms and then hook the wire back on to the straddle.

HUB-MOUNTED BRAKES

Hub-mounted brakes stop a bike by slowing down the speed of the hub. Regularly check disc brake pads for wear and alignment, replacing them when they are worn. Regularly check and replace the cables on cable discs and hub brakes. Examine the hoses of hydraulic brakes for leaks.

How they work

Hub-mounted brakes are activated by the pull of a lever on a cable, which causes pads to contact a braking surface. Springs push the pads away when the lever is released. In disc brakes, the pads act on discs attached to the hub.

In roller and coaster brakes, the pads act on a braking surface inside the hub. The action of the pads on the surface then slows down the hub and therefore the wheel. In hydraulic brakes, the lever's action pushes fluid through a hose; this fluid pushes the brake pads in the calliper into action. Of all the hub-mounted brakes, hydraulic disc brakes offer a rider the best control over the braking forces that can be applied.

Working in all weathers
An advantage of hub brakes over rim brakes is that their performance is largely unaffected by adverse riding conditions.

HYDRAULIC DISC BRAKE ANATOMY

When the rider pulls the brake lever, the hydraulic fluid in the hose pushes on the pistons in the calliper. These pistons in turn cause the brake pad on each side of the disc to contact the disc and to slow the rotation of the wheel. When the rider releases the brake lever, the pressure of the fluid in the hose decreases, allowing the springs (not visible) in the calliper to push the brake pads apart.

Hose
Contains fluid

Calliper
Contains pistons and two brake pads

Brake pad
Contacts the disc under pressure from the fluid

Disc
Slows down the hub of the wheel under pressure from the brake pads

Hose
Carries the brake fluid from the lever to the calliper

Brake lever
Compresses the brake fluid

HYDRAULIC BRAKE LEVER

Brake hoses are connected to a reservoir of brake fluid on each brake lever. The fluid fills the hoses all the way to the calliper on the wheel. Pulling the brake lever operates a piston in the reservoir, which pushes the fluid down the hose and, as a result, activates the calliper pistons.

Calliper
Houses the braking mechanism

Disc
Slows down the wheel

Cable disc brake

Cable disc brakes work well in all conditions. Even so, check the brake cables regularly for signs of fraying and keep them well lubricated. If the brakes do not release quickly when you let go of the brake lever, they need lubricating. Check brake travel, too, since excessive travel can mean that the brake pads are worn.

When you examine old brake pads, look at the way they are wearing. If they have developed a ridge, or the wear is in any way uneven, the calliper may need to be realigned.

When lubricating your bike, make sure that the lubricant does not fall on or touch the brake discs or pads. Do not even touch the disc or pad faces, because the grease from your fingers can easily affect their performance. Always clean the discs with methylated spirits.

STEP LOCATOR

Parts of a cable disc brake (front)

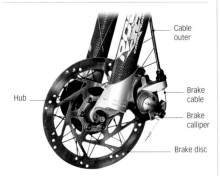

Cable outer

Hub

Brake cable

Brake calliper

Brake disc

Toolbox

- Allen key multi-tool ● Long-nosed pliers
- Cable pullers (optional)

Adjusting cable travel

1 **Loosen the cable-clamp bolt** on the calliper and pull through enough cable, with pliers or a cable-pulling tool, to take up any slack in the cable.

● Tighten the clamp bolt. This will reduce the travel on the brakes and is a necessary adjustment if the brake levers need pulling a long way before the brakes work.

Replacing pads

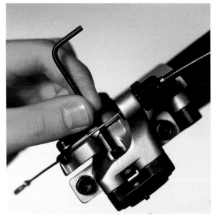

1 **Replace the pads** if the brakes are still not working effectively or if they are worn.

● Remove the spring clip with long-nosed pliers and loosen the pad-retaining bolt that holds them in the calliper. Take care not to damage the clips. The pads should now drop out.

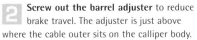 **Screw out the barrel adjuster** to reduce brake travel. The adjuster is just above where the cable outer sits on the calliper body.

• Loosen the fixing clamp to remove the old cable if a new cable is needed. Insert the new cable into the brake lever (see *pp.116–17*) and follow Steps 1 and 2 with the new cable.

• Lubricate the new cable before you fit it.

3 **Align the callipers** with the discs using the adjustment bolts. Undo these bolts, align the calliper so that its sides are parallel with the disc, and then tighten.

• Align brakes that are not equipped with this adjustment facility by using spacers to pack out the calliper-fixing bolts.

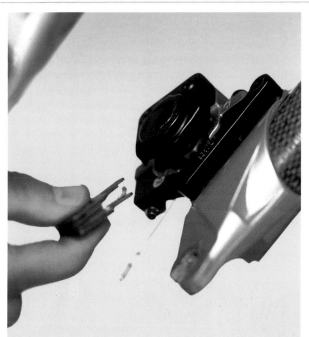

2 **Insert the new brake pads** and secure them with the Allen bolt and the spring clip.

• Clean your hands before handling brake pads as grease reduces the pads' ability to operate.

• Choose replacement pads that are specific to the manufacturer of the brakes fitted on the bike. Pads made from different compounds might be worth investigating if you want to alter the performance of your brakes.

Hydraulic disc brake I

Hydraulic disc brakes are more powerful than cable disc brakes, and once correctly installed, will require less maintenance. A bike that has disc-brake mountings on the frame and fork will be suitable for fitting a disc-brake system to.

Cable disc brakes can work with rim-brake levers but their performance falls fractionally short of hydraulic systems. These work by compressing a fluid rather than pulling a cable. Compatible hydraulic brake levers will need to be fitted to the handlebar and brake hoses that hold the brake fluid. Disc-specific hubs will also be required.

There is no need to fasten the front hose to the fork. To direct and keep the rear hose in place, use an adaptor kit to let the frame's cable guides take hoses, because the cable hole in a standard cable guide is too small.

STEP LOCATOR

Parts of a hydraulic disc brake

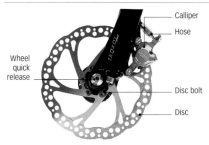

Calliper
Hose
Wheel quick release
Disc bolt
Disc

Toolbox
- Allen key multi-tool • Spanner • Stanley knife
- Thread-locking compound • Flat screwdriver

Installing a hydraulic disc-brake system

1 **Fit the calliper** using the Allen bolts and washers provided.

- Swap the washers around to pack out each calliper in order to line it up with the disc.
- Apply a thread-locking compound to the threads, then fix the disc to the hub using the disc bolts.

2 **Cut the hose** of the hydraulic system if it is too long by following Steps 3–7.

• Take out the brake pads (*see pp.128–29*) first and replace them with a spacer. The calliper used here is a demonstration model with no hose attached.

3 **Mount the brake lever** on to the handlebar and secure with the clamp bolts.

• Unscrew the aluminium shroud located where the hose joins the brake lever and move it out of the way. Prise open the brass olive beneath with a flat screwdriver.

4 **Move the brass olive** along the hose and out of the way.

• Prise the hose off the brake lever joint with a flat screwdriver, but be careful not to damage the lever joint. At the same time, gently pull on the hose to detach it.

5 **Carefully cut off** excess cable from the detached end of the hose with a sharp knife. Keep the olive and the shroud on the part of the hose that you will be reconnecting.

6 **Join the hose** to the brake lever by inserting it on to the lever joint. Push it home firmly, but not too hard as this can split the hose.

• Hold the hose upwards as you work to keep brake fluid loss to a minimum.

7 **Squeeze the olive** on to the hose at the lever joint to make a good seal.

• Screw the shroud on to the thread of the lever joint.

• Bleed the disc-brake system (*see pp.132–33*).

Hydraulic disc brake II

If you are pulling hard on the brake levers without much effect on the discs, or if you are pulling the levers several times to make the brakes work, you need to bleed air from the system. The following steps will also help if you have cut hoses to fit while installing a hydraulic system, had a leak in the system, or have fitted a new hose.

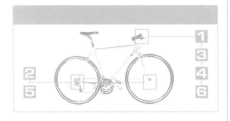

Toolbox
- Allen key multi-tool ● 10mm spanner
- Length of clear hose

4 **Angle the bike** so that the reservoir is level, open the bleed nipple and fill the reservoir with brake fluid. Pour with a smooth, constant stream to minimize air bubbles.

● Squeeze the brake lever all the way to the handlebar and hold it. Close the bleed nipple.

● Never mix brake fluids. Mineral oil or DOT 4 fluids cannot be interchanged.

Draining and replacing brake fluid

1 **Remove the wheels** from the bike to reduce the chance of brake fluid falling on the brake discs.

● Place a spacer in the calliper between the brake pads (see Step 2, p.131).

● Take off the brake fluid reservoir cover on the brake lever with an Allen key. Be careful not to let any of the brake fluid touch your hands.

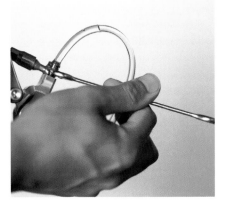

5 **Repeat Step 4,** filling up the reservoir until there are no more air bubbles flowing through the clear tube when you squeeze the brake lever. You will probably have to repeat this step four or five times before the bubbles in the tube completely disappear.

● Close the bleed nipple once the tube is bubble-free and the reservoir is full.

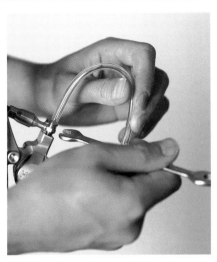

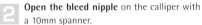 **Open the bleed nipple** on the calliper with a 10mm spanner.

● Slide one end of a short length of clear tube on to the bleed nipple.

● Put the other end of the tube into a plastic container that is big enough to collect the old brake fluid.

Pull the brake lever all the way back to the handlebar to remove some brake fluid.

● Tighten the bleed nipple.

● Make sure that all tools are to hand since the next steps require you to be organized.

● Cover the surface below where you are working since brake fluids can be corrosive. Use disposable mechanics gloves to protect your hands.

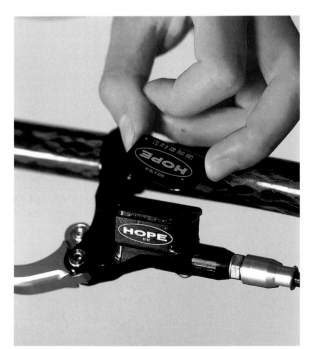

Replace the cover of the brake fluid reservoir but be careful not to displace any brake fluid.

● Refit your wheels and pump the brake lever a few times to centre the brake pads.

● Go for a flat test ride. If your brakes are not performing as they should there may still be air in the system. Repeat Step 4 and make sure that everything is tight.

Roller-brake cable

All brake cables wear out, no matter how much time is spent maintaining them. Cables for roller brakes – sometimes called drum brakes – are no different. If the bike is equipped with roller brakes, the steps in this sequence show how to replace a cable when it is frayed or worn out. However, lubricating the brakes and replacing the internal parts are occasional jobs that are best left to the experts at a good bike shop.

If the rear inner tube is punctured, or it is necessary to take off the back tyre to replace it, you need to know how to disconnect the rear brake in order to remove the back wheel. At the same time, you should know how to reconnect and adjust the brake after replacing the wheel. Once this is a familiar routine, it will also be possible to adjust the roller brakes for brake pad wear from time to time.

STEP LOCATOR

Parts of a roller brake

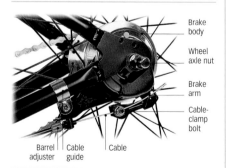

Brake body

Wheel axle nut

Brake arm

Cable-clamp bolt

Barrel adjuster | Cable guide | Cable

Toolbox
- Spanners
- Long-nosed pliers

Replacing a roller-brake cable

1 **Push the brake-arm cradle** towards the front of the bike. This takes the tension from the cable so that you can unhook the cable-clamp bolt from the cradle and remove the old cable.

- Screw the barrel adjuster on the brake arm in or out to about half of its extent.

- Remove the wheel at this point if you need to replace the tyre or inner tube.

4 **Tighten the cable-clamp bolt** while squeezing the cable slightly, as your helper keeps up the forward pull on the brake-arm cradle.

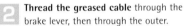 **Thread the greased cable** through the brake lever, then through the outer.

● Dribble a little oil into the outer.

● Make sure that the outer is firmly located in the lever, then thread the cable through the barrel adjuster and seat the outer firmly into it.

● Thread the cable through the cable-clamp bolt.

3 **Pull the cable backwards** with the long-nosed pliers while you push the brake-arm cradle forwards and hook the clamp bolt into it.

● Bend the cable slightly behind the clamp bolt and ask someone to push the brake-arm cradle forwards. Use your free hand to tighten up the bolt so the cable is nipped in place.

5 **Pull the brake lever hard** repeatedly (ten times) to bed in the brakes. The brakes may be a little tight as if they are being applied gently, even when there is no pressure on the lever.

● Keep about 15mm (²/₅in) of play in the brake lever before the brakes begin to bite.

6 **Screw in the barrel adjuster** a few turns until you achieve the 15mm (²/₅in) of play in the brake lever.

● Pull in the lever after each turn in the adjuster to check when the brakes begin to bite.

Coaster brake

Coaster, or back pedal, brakes are often fitted to children's bikes. They work, not by pulling a brake lever, but by the rider pedalling backwards. Their efficiency depends on the bike's chain having a very small amount of slack – about 3mm (⅛in) up and down is all that is allowed, otherwise the system does not work.

Mending a puncture or fitting a new tyre means disengaging the brakes and removing the rear wheel. This involves disconnecting the brake arm and putting the wheel back with correct chain tension. The job may be time-consuming but it is very important to do it properly. Use a workstand or simply turn the bike upside down and rest it on the handlebar and saddle.

If the rear wheel is removed during a ride because of a puncture, let the hub cool down for a few minutes before starting. The heat comes from the action of the brake pads on the internal braking surface.

STEP LOCATOR

Parts of a coaster brake

Drop-out

Hub

Gear satellite (other side)

Brake arm

Toolbox

- Spanners
- Screwdriver

Setting up a coaster-brake wheel

1 **Detach the brake–arm clip** from the brake arm by removing the clip bolt. When you reconnect the brake arm, make sure that this bolt is tight, because the brake arm acts as a counter-lever for the brake to push against.

- Hold the nut behind the arm with a spanner, while unscrewing the bolt.

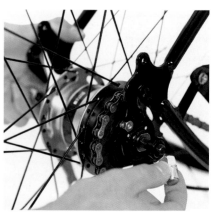

3 **Push the wheel forwards** and remove it from the drop-outs.

- Note the non-turn washer on the hub axle. This either screws on to the axle or sits on a flattened part of it, where its flattened profile or tab prevents the axle turning when the axle nuts are being tightened or loosened.

2 **Loosen the hub** of the coaster brake with two spanners of the correct size. The hub is secured in the frame drop-outs by two axle nuts, one on each end of the hub axle.

● Undo the axle nuts at the same time. When you remove them the wheel comes free from the frame.

4 **Lift off the gear satellite** as the axle clears the drop-outs. This connects the gear shifter to the gear mechanism through the control cable and butts up against the hub.

● Lift the chain off the sprocket to completely free the wheel.

● Lift the chain back on to the sprocket and replace the satellite before returning the wheel.

5 **Turn the axle** so that the flats or tab of the non-turn washer fits into the drop-outs, then replace the axle nuts.

● Pull the wheel right back, hold it straight and tighten the right axle nut, then the left one.

● Check the chain tension. If it is more than 3mm (¹/₈in) up or down, loosen the axle nuts, pull the wheel back and tighten the axle nuts again. Reconnect the brake arm by reversing Step 1.

6

TUNING YOUR

SUSPENSION

Suspension technology has revolutionized off-road riding. Accurate adjustment of the front fork and the rear shock allows uneven terrain to be tackled safely and confidently.

SUSPENSION FORKS

A suspension fork softens the blow of a bump on the road or trail. The fork must be checked for wear and lubricated regularly. The oil and springs should be changed either when they wear or to alter the characteristics of the fork.

How they work

The suspension fork on the front wheel absorbs the energy of a bump and prevents the force from reaching the rider. The fork's main spring, which can be trapped air or a metal coil, is compressed as the sliders move up the stanchions. Compression ends when the spring has absorbed the shock of the bump. At this point, the spring pushes the sliders back and the fork rebounds. Damping controls the speed of compression and rebound, usually by absorbing some of the energy of the bump with an air or oil damping mechanism. This creates friction, which slows down the fork's movements.

Reacting to bumps
Damping should prevent the fork from reaching the limits of its travel, but the fork should still be reactive enough to cope with every bump.

FRONT FORK COMPRESSION

Bunnyhopping gives a graphic demonstration of compression and rebound. As the rider picks up the front of the bike to clear the log, the fork rebounds because the rider's weight has been taken off the spring. On landing, the fork compresses as the spring absorbs the shock of the bike and rider landing.

Rebound

Pulling the handlebar upwards *and moving the body backwards lifts the front wheel so the front fork rebounds.*

Compression

Landing on the ground *returns the rider's weight to the bike's frame and compresses the front fork.*

AIR/OIL FORK

When a bump pushes up the sliders on this fork, a piston moves up the left stanchion, compressing the air. Once the bump has been absorbed, the air pushes the piston back and the fork rebounds. The damping mechanism in the right stanchion, which is full of oil, also moves up and down with the bump, controlling the speed of compression and rebound.

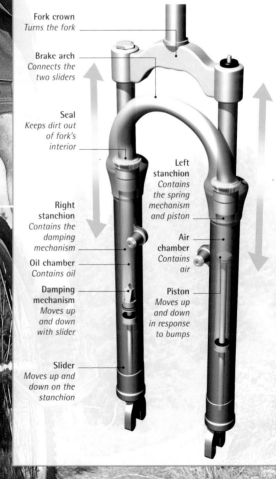

Fork crown
Turns the fork

Brake arch
Connects the two sliders

Seal
Keeps dirt out of fork's interior

Left stanchion
Contains the spring mechanism and piston

Right stanchion
Contains the damping mechanism

Air chamber
Contains air

Oil chamber
Contains oil

Damping mechanism
Moves up and down with slider

Piston
Moves up and down in response to bumps

Slider
Moves up and down on the stanchion

Front suspension

A suspension fork works best if it has been set up to accommodate the rider's weight. When you sit on your bike, the amount the fork depresses, as the slider moves down the stanchion, is called the sag. As you ride, sag allows the fork to extend into the hollows in the ground, giving a smooth ride. To set the amount of sag, you can increase or decrease the amount of pre-load in the fork.

Damping controls the speed at which a fork works. To find out if a fork is working too fast, lean on the handlebar, then quickly lift up the front of the bike. If the suspension fork bangs back to its limit, its action is too quick and its rebound damping needs to be increased. Adjust the damping still further after a few rides. The best set-up will see the fork absorb a hit and rebound quickly enough to be ready for the next.

STEP LOCATOR

Parts of a suspension fork

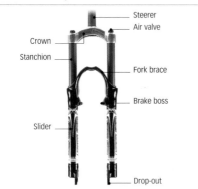

Steerer
Air valve
Crown
Stanchion
Fork brace
Brake boss
Slider
Drop-out

Toolbox

- Shock pump ● Tie-wrap
- Tape measure

Setting sag

1 **Put a tie-wrap** around the stanchion of the unloaded fork and next to the top of the slider. Ideally, the sag should be about 25 per cent of its available travel, though cross-country riders often prefer less and downhillers more.

3 **Get off the bike** and carefully measure the distance between the tie-wrap and the top of the slider.

- Express this measurement as a proportion of the fork's available travel. If the distance is 25mm (1in) on an 80mm (3¹/₅in) fork, the proportion is 32 per cent. Check the owner's manual to find out the available travel of your bike.

Fine-tuning the fork

2 **Sit on the bike,** wearing your normal cycling clothes.

● Place both feet on the pedals. Either ask someone to hold you upright on the bike or lean your elbow against a wall. The slider will travel up the stanchion, pushing the tie-wrap with it.

1 **Fine-tune the damping** on some forks with an adjuster at the bottom of one of the fork legs. The two air chambers in this fork enable further refinements to damping to be made.

● Pump air into the bottom chamber with a shock pump to change the spring characteristics.

● Change the size of a valve on the air piston to control air flow between chambers. This flow is called air-damping.

4 **Increase the air** in the chamber with a shock pump if the proportion of available travel is greater than 25 per cent.

● Increase the spring pre-load with a coil/oil system (there is usually a dial at the top of the fork leg) or fit stronger springs.

● Release air, reduce the pre-load or fit lighter springs if the proportion is less than 25 per cent.

1 **Make damping adjustments** on some types of fork while riding the bike. The controls for these on-the-fly adjusters are usually marked "faster" and "slower" to indicate which direction to turn them in. It is also possible to lockout some forks. This means that you can stop their action if you are riding over a very smooth surface and do not need suspension.

Coil/oil fork

If the sag has been set up correctly (see *pp.142–43*) but the coil/oil fork keeps bottoming out – the fork reaches the full extent of its travel but the spring cannot compress any more – it will be necessary to fit heavier-duty springs. Conversely, if the fork only reacts to the bigger lumps and bumps, lighter springs should be fitted.

The method of changing springs is similar in most coil/oil forks, but check the manufacturer's manual to find the features of the fork on the bike in question. It may not be necessary to remove the fork leg from the fork crown; or a spring in both legs of the fork may need replacing; or one leg may incorporate the spring, while the other has the damping mechanism.

STEP LOCATOR

Parts of a coil/oil fork

Steerer
Fork crown
Top cap
Fork crown bolts
Stanchion
Fork brace
Brake boss
Slider
Drop-out

Toolbox
- Spanner ● Allen key multi-tool
- Flat screwdriver

Setting up a coil/oil fork

1 **Remove the circlip** from around the rebound adjuster of the fork by prising it off with a flat screwdriver. Be very careful. Do not dig your screwdriver too far under the circlip, but put it far enough under so that it does not slip. Keep your fingers away from the screwdriver to avoid injuring yourself if it slips.

4 **Drop the new spring** into the fork leg. Make sure that it sits properly in the fork leg, then replace the top cap.

● Screw the top cap in with your fingers, then tighten it with a spanner.

2 Undo the retaining bolts in the fork crown so that you can drop the legs out. There are usually four retaining bolts. Some fork crowns do not have them, in which case undo a cap bolt at the top of the fork leg to remove the springs.

3 Start to remove the top cap of the fork leg with a spanner on the spanner flats, then unscrew the cap the rest of the way out with your fingers.

- Note how the spring is sitting in the fork leg, then lift the spring out.

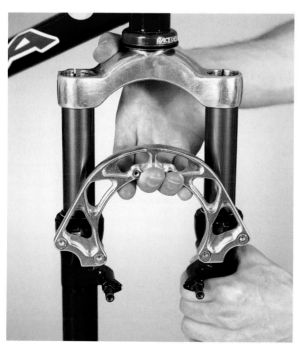

5 Put the fork legs back in the fork crown and secure the retaining bolts.

- Follow the manufacturer's torque settings when replacing the retaining bolts.

- Reset the sag of your forks (see pp.142–43).

Air/oil fork

Air/oil suspension forks usually have short travel and are popular with cross-country riders. Their spring medium is air, which makes them very light, and their mechanism is damped by oil.

Sometimes, they have a negative spring working in the opposite direction to the main air spring. This helps to overcome the stiction (the sticky friction between two adjacent but motionless objects) which is inherent in air/oil suspension forks and is caused by their very tight seals.

Changing oil is necessary from time to time, as dirt in the system starts to cause excessive wear. If you have increased the damping on your fork and its action is still too fast, replacing the oil with a heavier one will slow them down. In the same way, lighter oil can help to speed them up.

STEP LOCATOR

1 2 3 4 5

Parts of an air/oil suspension fork

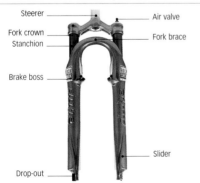

Steerer
Air valve
Fork crown
Fork brace
Stanchion
Brake boss
Slider
Drop-out

Toolbox

● Spanner
● Shock pump

Replacing oil

1 **Remove the cap** from the top of the stanchion without the Shrader air valve. This is the same sort of valve that is used on car tyres. You can carry out this following sequence of steps with the fork still in the bike, although it is easier if someone helps you.

3 **Make sure that you hold** the fork legs absolutely vertical.

● Place a bowl under the fork to catch any spillage. Carefully pour new oil into the stanchion until it is full and then replace the cap.

● Use a calibrated chemist's pouring vessel to ensure that you accurately measure the amount of oil the fork manufacturer specifies.

2 **Pour out the old oil** from the stanchion and collect it in a plastic cup. This air/oil fork has an open-bath damping system, where the damping rod moves up and down an open oil bath. The oil also lubricates the rest of the suspension system.

4 **Put the cap back** on the oil stanchion, tighten it and pump up the fork.

● Set the sag again (see pp.142–43), pumping air in or letting it out to obtain the ideal sag.

● Tighten the Schrader valve if, after setting up the sag correctly, your fork works well at first, then starts to bottom out (the valve may be leaking). Use a valve key from a car maintenance shop.

5 **Pump air in** or let air out of a fork with negative air springs after you have replaced the oil for one of a different viscosity.

● Adjust the damping of the fork so that it works at the speed you require, then fine-tune its action with the negative spring.

● Pump air in to make the fork more active over small bumps. Let air out to make it less responsive.

REAR SUSPENSION

The rear suspension absorbs the shock caused by a bump in the ground or rough terrain. A shock absorber must be kept clean and lubricated, and the bushings and frame mounts checked regularly for damage and wear.

How it works

The shock absorber of the rear suspension mirrors the specifications of the front fork in order to increase the rider's control of the bike. The rear triangle of the frame, which connects the rear wheel to the shock absorber, can move independently of the rest of the frame on bikes that are fitted with rear suspension.

Shock absorbers, or shocks as they are also known, consist of a spring medium, either a coil or trapped air, and a shaft. The shaft is usually connected to a damping mechanism, which contsins oil and controls the speed of the shock absorber's action.

COMPRESSION OF THE SHOCK ABSORBER

When the back wheel hits a bump on the road or trail, the rear triangle moves up on its pivots, compressing the spring, which absorbs the shock.

As the spring pushes back on the rear triangle of the frame, the shock rebounds, pushing the rear wheel back ready for the next bump.

When riding over smooth ground *the rear shock absorber is in a neutral position.*

When riding over rough ground *the rear shock is in a compressed position to absorb bumps.*

AIR/OIL SHOCK ABSORBER ANATOMY

In an air/oil shock absorber, the spring mechanism is compressed air that is sealed inside an air sleeve. The damping mechanism in the shock body contains oil. When the bike hits a bump, the shock body travels up inside the air sleeve and compresses the trapped air. Once this air spring has absorbed the energy of the bump, the shock absorber begins to rebound and return to its original position. The shaft, which runs from the top of the air sleeve into the shock body, is connected to the damping device. Oil flowing through holes in the device slows the action of the shock absorber in compression and rebound as the shock body travels up and down.

Bushing
Attaches shock to frame

Air valve
Controls air pressure in the sleeve

Rebound adjuster
Changes speed of rebound

Shaft
Runs into shock body

Air sleeve
Contains compressed air

Shock body
Contains the damping device

Rear shock
Absorbs the force of a bump

Rear triangle
Transmits the force of a bump to the rear shock

Rear wheel
Moves up and down in response to bumps

Rear suspension

A good-quality, full-suspension bike should be designed with a rear shock absorber that complements and works with the suspension fork in the front. Air/oil forks are normally accompanied by an air/oil shock and coil/oil systems are usually married together.

The first step in setting up a rear shock is to adjust its sag. Take into account the rider's weight, as with suspension forks (see pp.142–43), and then fine-tune its action by using damping and the shock's other functions after several rides on the bike.

One simple test to see if a rear shock is working in tune with the front fork is to press down on the middle of the bike, while looking at how the fork and shock react. For general riding, each should depress about the same amount.

Add the frame mounts, to which a shock is attached, to the routine safety checks (see pp.32–3). Check the bushes that allow the shock to pivot – consult the manufacturer's guide for instructions.

STEP LOCATOR

Parts of a rear suspension unit

Lockout lever   Air sleeve   Shock body

Rebound adjuster
Bushes

Toolbox

● Tape measure ● Shock pump

Adjusting the sag

1 **Measure the centre-to-centre distance** between the shock-mounting bolts with the bike unloaded.

● Sit on the bike and ask someone to measure this distance again.

● Express the second measurement as a proportion of the first. The figure should be between one quarter and one third.

3 **Accustom yourself to riding** a suspension bike before fine-tuning the damping speed with the rebound adjuster – if your bike has one.

● Turn the adjuster on an air/oil shock absorber but follow instructions on the shock to find out which way to turn.

● Do not set it too fast because this can upset the handling of the bike.

2 **Let air out** or pump it in as needed on an air/oil shock absorber.

● Take the second measurement again.

● Keep adjusting the air within the air/oil shock absorber until this measurement falls to where you want it within the recommended range.

● Increase or decrease the pre-load on a coil/oil shock absorber to achieve the measurement you want. Remember that the recommended range is only a guide.

4 **Undo the quick-release lever** (if your system has one) to alter the total amount of travel available, which can range from 87mm to 112mm (3½ in to 4½ in). This adjustment can be particularly useful at the start of a descent where increased speeds will mean bigger impacts from any obstacles you encounter on the trail. The increased travel will help to absorb them.

5 **Use the lockout mechanism,** if your bike has one, to stop the action of the suspension. The small blue lever on the illustrated unit will switch it on or off. Across flat ground, up a smooth climb, or on the road, the lockout temporarily prevents the suspension from absorbing the power you are putting into pedalling.

Glossary

Terms in *italic* within an entry are defined under their own headings within the glossary.

ALLEN BOLT A threaded bolt with a hexagonal depression in the centre of its head.

ALLEN KEY Hexagonal-shaped tool that fits *Allen bolts*.

BEARING A mechanism that usually consists of a number of ball-bearings and circular channels, or races. It allows two metal surfaces to move freely while in contact.

BLOCK Sprockets fitted to a *freewheel*.

BOSS Threaded metal fixture on a bicycle frame to which an item such as a bottle cage or a pannier rack is attached.

BOTTOM BRACKET Rotating unit that connects the *cranks* on either side of the bottom bracket shell to each other.

BOTTOM OUT A term that describes the point when a *suspension* fork or shock absorber reaches the limit of its *travel*.

BRAKE-LEVER HOOD The body in which the brake lever sits, connecting it to the handlebar.

BRAKE TRAVEL The distance a brake lever moves before the brake pads engage the braking surface on the rim or hub of a wheel.

CABLE TIDY A small, soft-metal cylinder that is closed at one end and fits over the cut ends of a cable to prevent fraying.

CASSETTE *Sprockets* that fit on the *freehub*.

CHAINRING A toothed ring attached to the *cranks* that drives the chain and, in turn, the *sprockets* and the rear wheel of a bicycle.

CHAINSET The assembly of *chainrings* and *cranks*.

CHAINSTAY The frame tube joining the *bottom bracket* shell and rear *drop-out*.

CLEAT A plastic or metal plate that fits to the sole of a cycling shoe and engages into a *clipless pedal* to hold the foot on the pedal.

CLIPLESS PEDAL A pedal with a mechanism to engage the *cleat* on the sole of a cycling shoe and hold it securely in place. Called clipless because they replaced pedals that had toe clips and straps.

COG A circular metal object with teeth, sometimes used as an alternative term for *sprocket*. It usually describes the parts within a hub gear that can be combined to give different gear ratios.

COMPRESSION The action of a *suspension* system when it absorbs an impact from the terrain. The term refers to the compression of the spring.

CRANK The lever that joins the pedals to the *chainrings* and transfers energy from the rider's legs into the *drivetrain* of the bike.

DAMPING The process that absorbs the energy of an impact transmitted through a *suspension* system. It controls the speed at which any form of suspension responds to uneven terrain.

DERAILLEUR GEARS A system that shifts the chain between *sprockets* on the rear wheel (rear derailleur) and between *chainrings* attached to *cranks* (front derailleur); it allows multiple gearing on bikes. See also *Mech*.

DOWN TUBE The frame tube that joins the *bottom-bracket* shell to the *head tube*.

DRIVETRAIN The assembly of pedals, *chainset*, chain, and *sprockets* that drives the bike forwards by transmitting leg power into wheel rotation. See also *Transmission*.

DROP-OUT A slotted plate at the end of the fork legs and stays, into which the axle of a wheel is attached.

EXPANDER BOLT A bolt that draws up a truncated cone or triangle of metal inside a metal tube in order to wedge the tube in place. Commonly found inside the stem of a threaded *headset*.

FREEHUB A mechanism, part of the hub, that allows the rear wheel to rotate while the pedals remain stationary.

FREEWHEEL A mechanism that does the same job as a *freehub* but can be screwed on or off the hub.

GEAR An expression of the *chainring* and *sprocket* combination, linked by the chain, that propels the bike.

GEAR-SHIFTER The control mechanism, usually on the handlebar, used to initiate gear-shifts.

GRUB SCREW A headless, threaded bolt that has a

single diameter throughout its length.

HEADSET The *bearing* unit that attaches the forks to a frame and allows them to turn. There are two varieties: threaded and threadless.

HEAD TUBE The frame tube through which the *steerer tube* runs.

HEXAGONAL BOLT OR NUT A threaded bolt with a hexagonal-shaped head, or a hexagonal-shaped nut that fits on to a threaded bolt.

HYDRAULIC A mechanical system that uses compressed fluid to move an object.

LOCKRING/LOCKNUT A ring or nut used to tighten on to a threaded object and lock it in place.

MECH Short for mechanism. Device that pushes the chain on to a larger or smaller *chainring* or *sprocket*. See also *Derailleur gears*.

NEGATIVE SPRING A device that works against the main spring in a *suspension* system. In compression, for example, a negative spring works to extend the fork, helping to overcome the effects of *stiction*.

NIPPLE The piece of metal attached to the end of a cable that secures the cable in the control lever.

PLAY A term to describe any looseness in mechanical parts.

QUICK-RELEASE MECHANISM A lever connected to a skewer that locks or releases a component from the frame.

REBOUND A term to describe the action of a *suspension* system after it absorbs an impact from the terrain. It refers to the extension of the system's spring.

SEAT POST A hollow tube that holds the saddle and is inserted into the *seat tube*.

SEAT STAY The frame tube joining the *bottom bracket* shell and rear *drop-out*.

SEAT TUBE The frame tube that holds the *seat post*.

SIDEWALL Part of the tyre between the *tread* and rim.

SPROCKET A *cog* turned by the chain. Combined with other sprockets, it forms a *cassette* or *block*.

STEERER TUBE The tube that connects the fork to the *stem* and handlebar.

STEM The component that connects the handlebar to the *steerer tube*.

STICTION A term that combines the words static and friction. It describes the tension between moving and static parts at rest, such as the seals and stanchions in a *suspension* fork.

STOPPER PIN The end of a cantilever or V-brake return spring that fits into a locating hole on the bike's brake mounting *bosses*.

SUSPENSION An air/oil or a coil/oil system that absorbs the bumps from a trail or road. The system is either integrated into the fork or connected to the rear wheel via a linkage.

THREADS The spiral grooves cut into metal that allow separate parts to be screwed or bolted together.

TOP TUBE The frame tube that joins the *seat tube* to the *head tube*.

TRANSMISSION A bike's transmission is made up of those parts that transfer the rider's energy into forward motion – the pedals, chain, *chainset* and *sprockets*. See also *Drivetrain*.

TRAVEL A term that refers to the total distance a component moves in carrying out its purpose. For example, travel in a *suspension* fork is the total distance the fork has available to move in order to absorb a shock. Brake travel is the distance a brake lever must be pulled before the brakes fully contact the braking surface.

TREAD The central part of a tyre that makes contact with the ground.

VISCOSITY A rating system for oils, which also refers to the weight. A light oil has low viscosity and moves quicker than a heavy oil through a given *damping* mechanism. This results in a faster-acting *suspension* system or reduced damping.

WHEEL JIG A stand that holds a wheel so that its rim runs between two jaws. Used in truing a wheel after replacing a broken spoke.

Index

Page numbers in *italic* indicate diagrams showing the location of parts and components. Page numbers in **bold** indicate entries where the maintenance of the part is the main subject on the page.

Acknowledgments

Author's acknowledgments

Pip Morgan and Richard Gilbert for their patient and diplomatic editorial work.

Ted Kinsey for designing everything so that the writing makes sense.

Dave Marsh of the Universal Cycle Centre for technical advice regarding road bikes.

Wayne Bennett of Don't Push It Mountain Bikes for advice regarding mountain bikes.

Tim Flooks of TF Tuned Shox for advice regarding suspension.

Gerard Brown for his excellent pictures and Guy Andrews for getting together the equipment we needed to show all the aspects of bike maintenance.

Jo Jackson and Keith and Barbara Oldfield for help when the author's computer broke down, twice.

Finally, all the bike companies who lent their equipment for our photoshoots.

Publisher's acknowledgments

Design: Janice English, Simon Murrell, Dawn Young

DTP Design: Gemma Casajuana

Photoshoot Art Direction: Jo Grey

Picture Research: Carolyn Clerkin

Proofreading: Lynn Bresler

Illustrations: Kevin Jones and Matthew White at Kevin Jones Associates, Tim Loughead at Precision Illustration Ltd.

Additional photography: Jill and Steve Behr at Stockfile

Models: Jay Black, Chris Hopkins, James Millard, Simon Oon, Helen Rosser, Rochele Whyte

Cycling models: Hsu Minh Chung, Jamie Newell, Claire Paginton, Hannah Reynolds, Simon Richardson, Kelli Salone, Ross Tricker, Russell Williams

Accessory, component, and bicycle suppliers:
Ian Young at Moore Large for Schwinn BMX; Caroline Griffiths at Madison for Profile, Shimano, Finish Line, Park, and Ridgeback; Ross Patterson and Jon Holdcroft at ATB sales for Electra and Marin bikes; Collette Clensy at Giant Bikes; Adrian at Pashley bicycles; Sean and Stuart at Evans Cycles, Wandsworth; Cedric at Luciano Cycles, Clapham; Sam at Bikepark, Covent Garden; Richard at Apex Cycles, Clapham; Graham at SRAM; Shelley at Continental; Trek UK.

PLEASE NOTE

Bicycle maintenance is potentially hazardous. Whilst the information in this book has been prepared with the reader's personal safety in mind, the reader may help to reduce the inherent risks involved by following these instructions precisely. The scope of this book allows for some, but not all, the potential hazards and risks to be explained to the reader. Therefore, the reader is advised to adopt a careful and cautious approach when following the instructions, and if in any doubt, to refer to a good bike shop or specialist.